Peace Be with You

Fr. Narciso Irala, S.J.

Peace Be with You

Keys for Coping with Anxiety, Sadness, Anger, and Doubt

Translated by Lewis Delmage, S.J.

SOPHIA INSTITUTE PRESS
Manchester, New Hampshire

Cover design by Perceptions Design Studio
in collaboration with Therese Blume.

On the cover: *The Storm on the Sea of Galilee* (1633) by Rembrandt van Rijn (DGX37B) © FineArt / Alamy Stock Photo.

Imprimi potest: James L. Connor, S.J., *Praep. Prov. Marylandiae*
Nihil obstat: James McGrath, J.C.D., *Censor Librorum*
Imprimatur: ✠ John Cardinal Krol, D.D., J.C.D.,
Archbishop of Philadelphia

Sophia Institute Press
Box 5284, Manchester, NH 03108
1-800-888-9344

www.SophiaInstitute.com

Sophia Institute Press® is a registered trademark of Sophia Institute.

paperback ISBN 978-1-64413-650-8
ebook ISBN 978-1-64413-651-5
Library of Congress Control Number: 2021953313

First printing

To all who would direct their feet
in the way of peace of heart
this book is earnestly dedicated

Contents

Translator's Introduction to the 1969 Edition

This post–Vatican II revised edition of Fr. Irala's book, further updated by the author, is, by our best calculation, its sixty-fifth edition. Over its publishing history of twenty-five years it has, in several languages, grown appreciably as a result of the author's added experiences, consultations, studies, lectures, and professional contacts.

The Second Vatican Council's *Gaudium et Spes* (Pastoral Constitution on the Church in the Modern World),[1] best of all modern documents, we think, describes the modern human situation which this book is designed to meet. In that document the value of human activity is gauged from the actual situation of men in the modern world. Human hope and anguish both grow out of profoundly changed conditions in the social order, changes which are psychological and moral as well as religious. Imbalances in the modern world relate to the broader desires of mankind and man's deeper questionings. Today reverence and love for human

---

[1] *The Documents of Vatican II*, edited by Walter M. Abbott, S.J., New York: America Press, 1966, pp. 199 ff.; esp. pp. 201–234, paragraph nos. 4–36.

dignity tie up with the interdependence of person and society, with the whole community of mankind, and promoting its common good.

A generation ago, the "Glacier-Priest," Fr. Bernard Hubbard, S.J., made the missions in Alaska known to hundreds of thousands of Americans by his slide lectures and color movies of mission life in Alaska. Some years ago, Fr. Irala began, as a kind of counterpart to Fr. Hubbard, lecturing in the Americas about the missions in China. He had had many years of experience in China, and later in Formosa, and so could portray factually and graphically many sides of mission activity. He traveled all over the United States and throughout Latin America as well. But Fr. Irala found that many people in our time felt a great need to solve personal problems. Indeed, these personal problems obscured their vision of larger human efforts both here at home and in fields afar. They would come in droves to hear about the workings of the human heart and emotions, how to use their minds more effectively, or about the daring pursuit of a noble ideal. They wanted to lead better lives and work for a better world. They were no longer so interested in seeing pictures of foreign lands or hearing about strange customs. "Here is a better approach," he said. "I will try to help people put to better use the great powers God has given them, their minds and hearts, their emotions and feelings, their enthusiasm. Then they will be better able to come in close contact with beauty and truth, goodness and grace. And so I may help open their minds and hearts to the great vision of humanity and of the work of Christ's Church."

Fr. Irala soon found he had to devote all his time and energy to these lectures and to personal consultations. Some personal problems, of course, needed specialized assistance. So they were referred to the proper clinics or doctors for diagnosis and therapy. But thousands of other problems were not in a category which demanded psychiatric assistance. Indeed, every teacher, doctor, parent, priest, or guidance counselor is regularly called upon to help with such problems.

Soon other priests, educators, and doctors demanded that he give his lectures a more permanent form by publishing them. He did so, and subsequent experience and consultations have resulted in revisions and additions to his book through sixty-four previous editions. These changes are included in this English edition. The chapter entitled "How to Rest" has been enlarged because of the enormous need of it; so many people are ignorant even of how to sleep right. And need has dictated the inclusion of a section on avoiding voice fatigue. The chapter "How to Think" has been dropped because it has been developed into a separate volume entitled *Mental Efficiency without Fatigue* (New York: Joseph F. Wagner, 1964).

Fr. Irala's original work, *O Contrôle Cerebral*, was first published at São Paolo, Brazil, in 1944. Shortly thereafter various foreign language translations appeared in Europe and Latin America and were as enthusiastically received as the original Portuguese edition. But the work was unavailable to English-speaking readers — an omission which this authorized translation has remedied.

The need for such a book is readily apparent. All of us at one time or another experience what — in the jargon of the psychologist — are called "personality maladjustments." These may be and usually are minor mental disturbances of one kind or another — doubt, worry, fear, and so forth — which, while not always requiring the specialized services of a psychiatrist, need very much to be corrected and avoided. To this end we need a practical handbook or manual that will outline an effective method of procedure. This translation of Fr. Irala's work does, we feel, more than adequately fulfill that need.

However, a word of warning may not be out of place at this point. Fr. Irala never intended this book as a panacea for all mental ills of whatever kind or degree. He does not pretend that the serious complications of a neurosis or psychosis admit of any facile solution to be found in the pages of this or any other manual. Special disorders must continue to require the attention of the specialist. But the ordinary, everyday problems of inefficiency, mental wandering, worry, overwork, insomnia, and loss of self-control, these he feels may be treated and an effective cure found for them in the manner here indicated.

The important thing is that Fr. Irala's methods have been found to work. His book is a manual of practice. It is meant, as the author himself says, not to be read on the run but to be studied and put into practice. Professional men who have read the manuscript—educators, guidance counselors, and directors of souls—have already testified to its effectiveness. But even more impressive has been the testimony of those who have personally profited from the author's work. Many of these actual cases are detailed throughout the text; many more have been by word of mouth; many, finally, have come to the author in a steady stream of letters and correspondence from all over the world. People who have never met him but who have read his book in Spanish, English, Portuguese, or Italian have written to ask his advice or to tell him how much he has helped them.

The author is, of course, a Catholic priest. His book is the product of years of experience both as a priest and as a practicing psychologist. It is a book, therefore, written out of knowledge and charity, and as such it will prove equally valuable to all—regardless of religious belief—who take it up in an awareness of their own need and with a true desire for self-help. For surely they are not only Catholics who experience bouts of depression; the experience is universal and has universal implications. All man's dreams and daring, all the richness of his emotional and affective life, all this forms a unity with his rational activity. Intellect and will are not discarnate. The whole man acts, thinks, desires, loves, hopes, and fears. All this human activity has been symbolized by the human heart—for, indeed, do we not say that a man is great-hearted, hard-hearted, chicken-hearted, weak-hearted? And for those who do believe, all man's ideals are symbolized and incarnate in the Heart of Christ. The peace of that Heart, which He would give to us, is there to be had, to be achieved. Fr. Irala outlines for us how many natural means, too, can help us to that supernatural goal.

There is a final note of caution needed for some readers. Let the reader *not* take from this book *only* the "natural" means which Fr. Irala suggests. Some readers can so "secularize" their use of this book as to pervert its intent. Their false starting point is to think that their personal problems can finally be solved apart from God. Such persons should perhaps begin their reading of this book with the footnote (Jung) on page 86, then chapters 14 and 15, and also pages 139-140.

—Lewis Delmage, S.J.

Preface

The dangers of the atomic age in which we live are outward signs of a still more terrible, because interior, explosive force. The mental life of modern man, his thoughts and impulses, his desires and feelings, his nervous breakdowns and chaotic hurrying and worrying: all these are more immediately threatening than atomic warfare.

Almost every month we discover new scientific, industrial, and political frontiers. We live in a day of atomic research, atomic explosions, atomic history. All the day long we are exposed to explosive impressions from newspapers, radio, TV, and the movies; in travel we ride the protracted explosion of jet planes; and we frequently find our business and social life building up frantically to an explosive potential. Everywhere we seem to have a thousand harrying details to attend to, and we find it harder and harder to live within the framework of twenty-four hours. All this exerts a fearful pressure on our interior life, so great a pressure indeed that to many of us our personal lives seem little more than one minor explosion after another.

Such is the experience, even in the most technologically advanced nations, of men of the highest ideals who have the best intellectual and managerial talent. American statistical sources speak of nineteen million persons needing sleeping pills every night. These are among the ten million diagnosed as neurotics and another twenty million without that official predicate. So many executives in business and industry have developed gastric or duodenal ulcers that this disease has been classified as an occupational hazard for them. There is so much hypertension and so many coronary illnesses among business executives that they are said to account for half of the total number of such cases.

In our thinking we no longer have that Socratic calm in which ideas follow one another in order. We have exchanged the Greek "sophrosyne," or classic poise, for a ragged horde of images and ideas. We lack the peace we need to concentrate our attention on one individual idea. From this come confusion, mental fatigue, nervousness, uneasiness, insomnia, and the like.

In our feelings, that moderation of our forefathers, as well as the healthy and holy gaiety of their family life, is yielding to abnormal or incoherent impressions, precocious or even brutal impulses, and exaggerated fears or desires. These become ingrained or magnified, or transfer themselves to undue objects. They give rise to all kinds of unreasonable fears (phobias), obsessions, anxieties, worries, and troubles.

In our decisions and goals we are no longer personalities with fixed norms to follow. Nor do we face the problems of life courageously and overcome its difficulties. On the contrary we find people without principles or strength of will, men and sometimes youths who are so disillusioned that they will even go to the extreme of committing suicide. They have a jumble of stray impulses and foolish desires which come from outside stimuli or unchecked instinct. These take the place of deliberate decision governed by reason and go on to produce indecision, loss of willpower (abulia), inconstancy, and discouragement. Finally the higher level of consciousness loses control of the impulses which come from its lower subconscious levels. And the will loses control over the drives toward mere sense pleasure.

Too frequently life turns out to be agitated and restless, amusing, if you will, but sad and empty, tormented, anarchical. For some it is living without knowledge of how to rest peacefully or work efficiently. For others it is ignorance of how to have a real desire, or how to dominate feelings or the sexual instinct. For many it is a life empty of interior happiness and, at least for some, merely a heap of diversions and pastimes.

This book has been written in the hope of alleviating, in some part, such burdens and to give some guidance in the re-education of control. It is primarily the fruit of the author's own personal experience.

In the first place it is meant for those who are fatigued from excessive work, worries, or sufferings. Possibly they may have lost control of their thoughts and so will not know how to rest or sleep peacefully; or they may be unable to control their fears or sadness. The first part of the book is intended especially for this group.

Secondly, we are writing for those who are healthy of mind but who wish greater efficiency in studies or business, greater energy and constancy in carrying out plans, greater control of feelings or instincts, more joy, satisfaction, and interior happiness. These will find useful and practical advice especially in the second part of the book.

Further, we are also writing for educators and directors of souls who meet up with problem cases regarding study or virtue. These problems often arise because of mental wandering, inefficiency, indecision, or even laziness of will. Difficulties may also come from uncontrolled passions, unreasonable fears, or feelings of inferiority.

In the arrangement of the book our purpose is first of all to be practical, to make it easier for you, our readers, to get quick control of your nervous and mental energies. The upshot of this will be greater efficiency in work and greater mental health. We want also to be accessible, even for non-specialists, in order to lessen mental sufferings and help those who need orientation or advice in their work or studies. We want, too, to save time for you. Hence we unify our teachings, condense explanations, make résumés of them, and include outline diagrams or charts at the end of each chapter. We want, further, to focus your attention especially on mental fatigue, mental weakness, insufficient control, and the internal difficulties which these cause. In practical applications we limit ourselves to the more immediate results of acquired control. And, finally, we want to interweave aphorisms or maxims which are educative and healthily optimistic. Once you engrave these on your mind by repetition, they will help to increase your health, efficiency, and happiness.

Peace Be with You

Part 1

Happiness and
Our Equipment for It

1

False and True Happiness

Before we go into the practical means of increasing happiness, or removing obstacles to it, we should first look at what happiness is. This chapter, necessarily abstract, is a guide to the concrete techniques which come later.

We should of course bear in mind that the happiness of this life is necessarily limited and imperfect. But though we are, in this book, seeking no earthly utopia, we must admit that much of our "unhappiness" is self-made and unnecessary, much of it the outcome of seeking a false "happiness."

On the façade of the palace of pseudo-happiness we read invitations to pleasures, riches, fun; but happiness is not there. Echoes whisper to us from deep in its interior: "Emptiness, upset, disgust." Riches do not satisfy; they did not satisfy the eighty millionaires who committed suicide in the United States in one year. Nor should we confuse pleasure with happiness. By equating them, many have surrendered to vice, and found degradation, disgust, sickness, remorse, premature death, and a likelihood of eternal damnation. Amusements and rounds of entertainment promise but do not bring us real fulfillment.

There are so many young people who live without an ideal and feel deeply the emptiness of their lives. They would have done well to fill their lives with the satisfaction of duty done, or sacrifice for a noble cause. But they are satisfied to mask it with a series of amusements or drown it in coarse laughter or wild excitement. None of these roads lead to happiness.

True happiness is like a noble lady, calm and collected, who dwells in the interior of the soul's castle, knowing her real treasures and growing in appreciation of them. She is often seen externally through the window of the face when she clothes the human face with a smile. Her smile is the bright vesture of a rational being, something had neither by the animals nor the most beautiful flowers.

True happiness hides from us whenever we go after it out of egoism or devotion to our own personal convenience. But it comes running to meet us whenever we put self aside and, embracing what is noble, devote ourselves to duty, virtue, the good of our neighbor, and God. External events scarcely affect this at all. These can certainly upset us if we meet them unwisely.

But an intelligent appraisal of our external life situations should bring us resignation, peace, and joy instead of resentment, upset, and melancholy. The wise and happy person discovers the inner meaning of everything and every situation. He relates its value to the help it can give us in glorifying our infinitely good Creator and attaining another eternal and perfect kind of happiness.

In this description we distinguish happiness (which is an intimately personal thing, tranquil, deep, and based on a certain nobility) from an alleged happiness which is really false, turbulent, and base. In it we list its three psychical elements: the factors of thought, will, and feelings. And we mention its physiological counterpart, the human smile. Now to explain this briefly and summarize it in a schematic formula.

Happiness is *noble*. True satisfaction is not to be found in vice, anything degrading, or any illicit pleasures. Fast upon the sparkling sensation follows a lasting and bitter emptiness. And the deep-rooted longing for moral greatness is inhibited or cancelled out. It is not built upon riches, pleasures, or power. Often there is more peace and joy among the comparatively poor than among the rich and the mighty. Many millionaires, crushed with worries, have grown old before their time.

Happiness is *altruistic*. And it seems to play hide-and-seek with us. A day spent in pleasure-seeking at our own caprice leaves an emptiness behind in us. But a day of sacrifices for God or neighbor results in deep satisfaction.

Happiness is *calm and collected*. There is no happiness in agitation and chaos. Happiness is found in the innermost part of a rational being. It is a deep satisfaction and unshakable peace.

Happiness is not caused by external events. For the same outcome may bring resignation, peace, and joy to some, and sad despair to others.

The lady of the castle knows and appreciates her real treasures and increases them. Here we have the three psychical factors in true happiness. The first factor has to do with our *mind* or *thoughts*. By it we know or think about the great good had or soon to be had by us, and about the ways to increase it. The second factor is *volitional* or *executive*. By love, action, and decision we preserve and even increase that treasure. The third factor is connected with our *feelings and emotions*. By it we feel and appreciate our treasures. (Chapters 3, 4, and 5 follow from this.)

The above we reduce to an outline diagram as follows:

1. Happiness Formula

Prerequisite: A treasure possessed or assured.

Constituents: Thought about "the treasure"
Love of it and the will to hold and increase it
Feeling of satisfaction in it

Fulfillment: The external expression of joy: a smile

2. Happiness Formula

To live: Beauty, truth, goodness, grace

In the present: Not the past or the future

With unity: Of thought and action

And fullness: Of satisfaction, peace, and security

Happiness is a matter of *living*, really living. The nobler and more active the life, the greater its happiness. For man is an animal capable of desire. He can discover higher goods and desire them, too. His true life, and the noblest of his activities, consists in knowing which goods or treasures can really satisfy him, in working to attain them, then enjoying their possession. His ideal is not a kind of Buddhist Nirvana which offers deification but mutilates the life of the spirit and annihilates all personal activity. That kind of negative annihilation of desire is really an impoverishment. True happiness, however, is that of heaven. Yet to a lesser degree there is also true happiness to be had on earth. We experience it when we possess divine and human goods or treasures in such a way that they fulfill our aspirations and absorb our consciousness. What they annihilate are sad thoughts of the past and dread of the future. And so they make impossible any desire other than the happiness presently possessed. This is another, a positive kind of annihilation; it implies possession of everything we want. Life in the present is a treasure possessed, and future life a treasure to be had, one we need to make us truly happy. For its sake we can take possession of the world of color, shape, and sound; the world of friendship and society; of science, beauty, love and, above all, of the supernatural treasures which God has deposited in His Church.

We must live *beauty*. Let it enter deep into us and impress itself on our affections and feelings. To this end we must receive sensations with full consciousness. They will give us an *aesthetic* happiness. (See chapter 3, "Receptive Activity.")

We must live *truth*. The more knowledge we gain and the deeper and clearer our understanding, the less fatigue we feel and the more intellectual satisfaction we experience.

And we must live *goodness*. This is an active process—loving others and making them happy, loving God above all. There is also a passive aspect to it: feeling the love and goodness of others, and the love of God pouring itself out upon us.

Finally, for those of us who have faith, we must live the life of grace, activate it, increase it. The life of grace divinizes us and makes us able to do what is more than human, able to attain a happiness which is more than human, somehow divine.

We must live in the *present moment*. This is the only moment within our hands, the only one that can make us happy. The past exists no more; let us leave it to the divine mercy. And, though it does not yet exist, let us entrust the future to God's loving providence and live happily in the present. The present is a narrow track drawn between two "chasms"—the past and the future. If a man falls by sadness or scrupulosity into the past or sinks by worry into the future, he stops advancing toward his happiness.

We must live the present in a *unity* of thought and action. Mental unity and concentration bring efficiency and joy (chapter 3). Whenever a man has many things to think about or do at the same time, he becomes nervous, upset, worried, but not happy.

Above all we must live in the present with a *fullness* of satisfaction, peace and joy. When the present does not give us such fullness, as when seeking pleasure, wealth, or power (these fulfill only our lower aspirations), we experience a tendency to long for the past or dream about the future. Then the past or future occupies the mind and robs it of happiness. For the "poorness" of the present cannot absorb all our interest and attention. However, if the value of the present does satisfy our most noble aspirations, then our consciousness is filled with it and enjoys it and does not look to or hang upon the past or the future.

Mystics enjoy such moments of full living when grace suspends the operation of their senses. To a lesser extent a parallel exists in the case of any spiritual consolation (e.g., when we feel united to God in fervent prayer). An experience somewhat resembling this is had in moments of poetic inspiration or during a musical concert; also, in scientific intuition and when discovering some new truth; in pure and sincere love; while bringing happiness to our neighbor; in the satisfaction of duty done; and while carrying out what we know to be the will of God.

These happy moments of ours are an imperfect experience if they are not based on a pure and peaceful conscience and a sense of security in possessing them. The repetition of such "full" present moments, and prolonging them, brings us true, though limited, happiness in this life. And this is as deep a happiness as can be had in this life. And it can be had even in the midst of sorrow or pain. This will become, in the next life, completely full and limitless, without any possibility then of suffering.

But these two happiness formulas are impossible for those who look for happiness in vice, vanity, or disorder. These formulas are difficult for many victims of the lack of control in modern life.

2

Re-education for Happiness

Whoever looks for happiness where it is not to be found – in vice, vanity or disorder – will have to begin by adjusting his life to the ways of duty and virtue. Books about morality and the life of the spirit will teach him how to do this, especially if he also gets personal advice from some head wiser than his own. In this book we aim to help the many people of good will who actually are on the right track but are not so happy as they should be. Either they do not understand or do not use correctly the mental (psychical) equipment which would give them unity and fullness of life at the present moment.

Some lack a clear precision in their use of the senses. They do not pay real attention to what they see or do. So they block off from entering within them the peace and joy of really conscious sensations or aesthetic pleasure. Others subject themselves to excessive fatigue. Others let their mental life go wandering all over the place. So they find no rest or depth in their thoughts. And they do not experience the joy and efficiency that would come from orderly mental work. Still others are indecisive or fickle. They do not know how to use the immense force of their will. Finally, many others experience antipathies and repugnance, attractions and inclinations that obsess them and draw them still further away from duty. Or the breakdown of their emotional life is seen in excessive feelings of sadness, fear, or disgust. The conclusion of all this is that we have to know how to use these factors in the life of our spirit correctly. Control in the use of them will increase our happiness.

The following paragraphs on emotional machinery give more details about the symptoms, causes, and remedies for this lack of mental and emotional control which blocks happiness. In such a brief outline there is no attempt to include the whole sweep of the problem of psychical or psychosomatic troubles. Still less does it mark out the frontiers between the physical and spiritual; so often these overlap and intermix. What follows is a pedagogical outline of the sufferings which are a consequence of insufficient control. It is a bird's-eye view of the problem.

Important notice to the reader: Before you look over the following schematic outline, first let me ask you a question. When you hear illnesses described, do you tend to fear or find the same symptoms in yourself? If so, skip the next few pages. Or read them if you wish, but only if you also go back and go over the first part of this book again. Or at least bear in mind that, if you do have some of these symptoms yourself, that is no sign of abnormality and, still less, of an illness which is dangerous or difficult of cure. Almost all of us have had or will have some kind of weakness or lack of control. A great psychiatrist at the University of Bogota would exempt from such defects only Jesus Christ and His Blessed Mother. So be not apprehensive and, as you look over these pages, do not expect to find out that you are sick. Rather, look for your own *greater* health, efficiency, and happiness. Then the following outline will help you to focus on and remedy the little you lack. It will also help you to understand other people better.

Symptoms of Fatigue, Insufficient Control, or Psychosomatic Illness

A *list of somatic symptoms*

Feelings of heat or heaviness in the head, or headache. Muscular tension with little or no relaxation. Nervousness while awake or at bedtime, and frequent waking at night and trouble going back to sleep. Feelings of fatigue and incipient dizziness. Excessive blushing without reason. Difficulty with speaking in public. Hypersensitive hearing. Trouble with breathing, digestion, circulation, etc., etc.

A *list of psychical symptoms*

In one's ideas or imagination: Fixed ideas (usually depressing) linked with feeling dispirited, scrupulous, persecuted, fearful, worried, etc.; or *fixed trains of thought* (uncontrolled or uncontrollable): the day's impressions run through one's mind like a movie, continual distractions, difficulty paying attention, lessening or loss of memory.

In conscious life: lack of objectivity, of clear consciousness, or of adequate response to impressions received. A victim of this escapes from reality and from society into egocentrism. *He neither lives in nor enjoys the present;* he does not pay full attention to what he sees or hears. *He lives in the past or the future,* far away from his physical location, wrapped up in sadness, scruples, or worries. He daydreams. An excessively subjective life.

In the feelings: impressionability, irritability, excessive and persistent fears or desires. He feels disgusted, or anxious, or alternates between feelings of sadness and joy, peace and turmoil, enthusiasm and discouragement, all without objective cause.

In the will: indecisiveness, abulia, instability, lack of perseverance. *The sufferer acts on impulse rather than deliberately.* Consequently there is a feeling of inferiority or inability, and various fears. *He is a prisoner in his own jail.*

In a word, there is a painful duality and a random kind of activity, a loss or lessening of self-control.

To comprehend the foregoing better, a good procedure will be to enter into the psychology of victims of the illness by listening to their own description of it. (Three case histories will shortly follow and more of them will be found throughout the book.) Unfortunately in the accelerated life of our age these victims are legion. They are recruited daily and not very often found among intellectual or affective nonentities. For these latter do not usually have the exuberance of mental life that is a prerequisite of swinging to an extreme and losing control. More often we see them among thinkers, writers, and men of arts, among persons of exquisite sensibilities, among ambitious and talented students. How many lecturers, writers, and professors of international fame have in our day been struck down by overwork! Darwin, for example, admitted that he could not work more than two hours a day. Even Dr. Vittoz, the psychotherapist, began by curing himself. And so it should not be a shameful or depressing thing to declare oneself mentally fatigued.

"At the age of twenty," a student describes himself, "despite an insatiable love of books, I suddenly found it impossible for me to study. Ten minutes of reading or writing brought on the most distressing feeling of fatigue. There was pain and, more frequently, a feeling of heat around the head and eyes. I simply could not drive off this sensation and concentrate on other ideas. A confusing succession of thoughts so oppressed me that I did not know how to control them. They were usually sad memories of the past, or painful anticipations of future misfortunes. They were sometimes so burdensome that I could not wholly drive them away by seeking refuge in conversation, walking, or even manual labor. The most intimate part of my soul seemed split in two. I felt as if another part of me were overcoming the conscious part of me. Gradually I sank into discouragement, worry, feelings of inferiority, and indecision. At times there was a swift transition from optimism to pessimism, from joy to sadness, without any objective cause. I was on an open road to all sorts of phobias, fear of appearing in public, incipient dizzy spells, and scruples of conscience.

"A little later I fell prey to insomnia. My time of rest brought me no true repose. My sleep was interrupted by dreams and nightmares. When I got up I would find that I was more tired than when I went to bed. The illness and my sadness increased, yet those closest to me misunderstood it. When they saw me apparently strong and physically robust, some diagnosed that the illness came from my imagination. Others more charitably, but not more scientifically, tried to persuade me to do what I so anxiously wished to do, that is, not to be worried, not to be absent-minded, not to fear, to control myself. But they did not show me *how* to do it. It was as if you were to advise a person suffering from a fit of coughing or vomiting simply not to cough, not to vomit, without telling him the means to employ.

"I went through ten years of this. But after six months of exercises for mental re-education I triumphed over all those difficulties. Now I have almost forgotten that I had been ill. Although I have not yet recovered the same full capacity for work as heretofore, I do find that I am cured and satisfied."

I, too, the author, had to pass through that sorry state of distressing introspection. Yet it was useful. For my own pattern of mental activity was developed and illuminated first by the knowledge and advice of the famous Jesuit psychologist Fr. Laburu.[2] It was afterward completed and systematized in Lausanne by Dr. Arthus, according to the precepts of Dr. Vittoz.

They gave me the key to my cure in the re-education of control. This method I have confirmed by study and wide experience with the sick. It has taught me how to direct and console those who are suffering from illnesses similar to mine. I say "to direct and console," for we should not prescind from medical aid. Even if symptoms seem to be alike, they sometimes have far deeper roots. In such cases only consultation with a spiritual psychiatrist could promise security and improvement.

"I am eighteen years old," a student once wrote to me, "and formerly I was as strong as an oak. I could read for hours and hours without fatigue. I was very optimistic and felt capable of any undertaking. But last term I studied very little and had a lot of fun with various companions. As examination time drew near we spent several nights studying until three o'clock in the morning. We drove off sleepiness by means of coffee. But now that the examinations are over,

[2] Professor of Scientific Questions at the Gregorian University (Rome).

I hardly know what has happened to me. Sleep is a torment. It is either a network of images or else a single image which continually repeats itself. Even during the day my head boils. I cannot pay attention to conversation. Reading tires me. I cannot distract myself. Life terrifies me; I am afraid of everything, even of myself."

This young man lost control because of excess disorder in his mental work. Let such a one take heart, begin to strengthen his overexcited nervous system, perhaps travel a bit and rest. Then let him begin the work of mental re-education. Let us form ourselves without waiting for somebody else to form and model us. See, for example, how children amuse themselves when they are alone. They build structures of clay or sand which they then enjoying leveling to the ground; so should we in solitude mold our characters and virtues, and destroy our defects.

Four everyday duties will help me to achieve a healthier mental life. I must resolve, first, to strengthen and govern my body (nourishment, exercise, and discipline); secondly, to feed and enlighten my intellect (serious, concentrated work); thirdly, to elevate and control my heart (love of God and neighbor); and finally, to strengthen and exercise my will (decision and constancy).

3

Receptive and Productive Mental Activity

In order to attain mental mastery **man should be** capable of governing the kingdom of his mind, of opening or shutting its gates by receiving or rejecting thoughts at will. This mental activity is twofold: the mind receives sensations like a photographic camera or radio receiver, in which case the attention is gentle and almost passive; but it also produces images, ideas, and reasoning processes like a movie projector or radio transmitter. Whether these are consciously or unconsciously elaborated, this is active or creative attention.

We base re-education upon the distinction between the receiving and producing powers of our mental world. Our axiom is that we cannot be fully both receiving and producing at the same time.

Receptive Power

Receptive power is exercised when we receive conscious sensations. This means not only to stimulate our senses through noise, smells, hardness, and so forth, and to send nervous currents to our brain centers, but also to put more life into our sensations, receiving them consciously and filing them away in memory.

When distractions do not frustrate them from without and our secret thoughts do not tamper with them from within, conscious sensations are a tonic for the brain and the nervous system. They bring peace, joy, tranquillity, and repose. They allow nature to work. Through them the objective world created by God enters within us with all its beauty. For if you know how to receive it within yourself, you will obtain joy from the blue of the sky, peace of a starry night, beauty and variety of flowers, freshness of morning air, whisper of a fountain, whistling of wind, greenness of fields, trilling of birds, songs of innocent children.[3]

Re-education of Receptive Power

Many persons rarely have clear sensations. This is especially true of the emotionally disturbed. They live in their own subjective world which is sad and unreal. Only rarely do they come out into the exterior world, beautiful and joyful as it was created by God. And even when they do, their sensations are modified by extraneous or subjective thoughts. To these people we offer the following advice.

For your re-education you should apply your sense of sight for about ten or twenty seconds to a landscape, an object, a detail. Keep a tranquil or almost passive attention. Take your time. Consider the object before you and no other. Pay no

---

[3] "This world in which we live needs beauty in order not to sink into despair. It is beauty, like truth, which brings joy to the heart of man and is that precious fruit which resists the wear and tear of time, which unites generations and makes them share things in admiration." *Documents of Vatican II*, op. cit., p. 732 (Closing Message to Artists).

attention to any other idea. Let the object enter within you as it is in itself, without any special effort. Look at it the way a young child does. Take care that the muscles of forehead and eyes are loose and relaxed. When your nerves and muscles are tense, it is easy to have mental tension also. This results in lack of peace in the act of vision. But if your muscles relax, your mind also tends to rest.

Apply your hearing to a near or distant noise. Let yourself be penetrated by the sounds as above, naturally, without mental discussion of the fact or its cause. Be a mere receiver of sound and perceive it with pleasure and relaxation.

Apply touch by feeling objects, their coldness, heat, hardness, and so on. Feel your own footsteps, the chair on which you are resting, the door opening. Feel your own breathing, the air entering your chest and filling it. The first sensation perceived will be the most conscious.

At first it is not so easy to practice these fully conscious sensations with no attention at all paid to anything else. So, in your first attempts, you might find yourself thinking about the process itself, or the cause, effect, or some circumstance, instead of *what* you perceive. But in a few days, after a series of good tries, you will succeed in separating the pure sensation from accessory mental processes. And then you will find joy and rest in the sensation itself.

> Attention! *The exercises proposed in this chapter should not be done in such a way as to produce tension, worry, or obsession with them. On the contrary, they should help us achieve peace and optimism. They are a kind of psychic gymnastic and they will, indeed, help us if we do them with progressive naturalness and ease.*

Walking consciously. This exercise is very useful for resting as well as for overcoming agoraphobia (that is, a morbid fear of crossing an open space or being out in the open). It also counteracts attacks of incipient dizziness. Hence we shall describe it in greater detail.

First get a separate sensation or clear consciousness of your foot being put down, your leg moving and your whole body sliding forward. Then coordinate these sensations and unite them to the rhythm of your breathing and to visual and auditory perception. You will then have a feeling of freedom and security.

Practicing conscious sensations. If you are haunted by these troubles or by dizziness, exercise yourself in these sensations several times morning and afternoon. Do them, for example, on five different occasions. Each time spend about five minutes on them and receive five or more sensations through each sense.[4]

Try to experience, as far as possible, the truth in the old maxim *"Age quod agis,"* that is, "Attend to what you are doing," or "Do what you're doing." But you must do all this as if in sport, with no anxiety, fear, or worry.

In a few days you will notice a greater peace and joy. The world will appear more beautiful. It will, as a matter of fact, impress you as it really is in itself. It will not be colored by your uncontrolled unconsciousness.

A very depressed person once made this statement to me: "After ten days of conscious sensations I feel myself another

---

[4] Follow the same norm in the concentration and will exercises. Do them the same number of times morning and afternoon. Each time do each exercise about five times in order to form a healthy habit.

man. The world seems joyful and beautiful to me." Previously he had been looking at it through the prism of his sad thoughts. Or rather, he had been looking at it, but had not seen it. Many people have been cured by this exercise alone.

Chinese painters, we are told, retire to a mountain before actually painting in order to contemplate and feel nature. They let it enter into themselves in all its beauty. Afterward they transfer it to their canvas just as they sensed it. That is why their pictures have so much life and feeling. To allow exterior beauty to enter into oneself is characteristic of painters and poets.

Productive Power

Under this heading we include ideas, images, associations of ideas, and reasoning processes. These may be produced voluntarily or spontaneously by the unconscious. This "production" is active attention, work. This is the normal cause of fatigue which varies according to the kind of concentration.

Concentration

When we follow the course of one idea to the exclusion of every other, when we are attentive only to what we are studying or hearing and forget everything else, even ourselves, then the intellectual return is at its maximum. Then natural pleasure is great, and there is only that minimal fatigue which we call physical. Two hours of this perfect attention are equalized by five minutes of rest through conscious sensations ("receiving"). A day's work is balanced by a night's sleep. Thus we can work intensely at a single idea for many years, and intense and orderly study, far from weakening the brain, is a gymnastic which strengthens it.

Imperfect attention. Our attention is poor when we follow out one idea with another idea or image constantly interrupting it. This we call a distraction. Then the return and satisfaction are less and fatigue greater.

Our attention is harmful to us when we follow out several ideas simultaneously. This happens, for example, when we are reading or listening to an explanation or discourse and at the same time we attend to another parasite idea (worry, fear, sensation of fatigue, scruples). The fatigue is then disproportionate, abnormal. We call this mental fatigue. Then we grasp ideas less deeply and forget them sooner. The distraction, or parasite idea, has an effect like that when two typewriter keys are both touched at the same time. The machine resists and the writing is confused. So our brain becomes fatigued and we understand ideas but poorly, and we can have no experience of satisfaction or joy. A quarter of an hour's work is not equalized by another quarter hour's rest. A whole night is not enough to make up for the day's expenditure of energy. This is why we are exhausted from a hurried visit to a museum or after nervously rushing through the newspaper. If this type of labor is continued it leads at last to "overwork" (fatigue of the brain) and "breakdowns."

Geniuses of one sort or another—artists, inventors, heroes, saints—are usually silent, concentrated. Dissipation weakens by dispersing energies; concentration gathers them together, as it were, in a close bundle.

According to a new theory, imperfect concentration is often responsible for some visual defects or indistinct vision due to bad focusing. When the accommodation nerves of the eyeball are taxed by divided or imperfect attention, they put into a state of excessive tension the muscles which lengthen or shorten for the purpose of focusing upon the object. With time these muscles lose the elasticity which is necessary for accommodating the eye to vision.

That is the reason why many nervous people, by practicing *"Age quod agis"* ("Do what you're doing"), improve their concentration and often find that their vision also is bettered.

Causes of Defective Concentration

1. Bodily weakness
2. Nervous and muscular tension
3. Lack of training or bad training of the attention
4. Some emotional disturbance, a fear or desire which pulls all thought into its wake (this is the most frequent cause)

Re-education of Productive Power

In addition to strengthening of the body to counteract weakness, and relaxation exercises to counteract tension, re-education will be twofold. One phase will be more mechanical and technical, the other more mental. Let us take up the former first.

Everyone, even the mentally ill, can concentrate his attention for a moment of time. Beginning with this possibility and graduating the exercises, he can arrive at normal concentration.

The exercises here proposed are not the only ones nor are these particular exercises absolutely necessary. But they have as guarantee the experience of the old school of psychotherapy at Lausanne. They may be omitted by persons whose problem is not one of increasing the productive power of concentration or by those for whom the exercises of conscious sensations, as outlined previously, suffice. Whatever other method may help the victim to get out of himself and fix his attention on other ideas will be advantageous. This will be especially true if he finds it useful and pleasant.

External visual concentration. If you make a dot and think of nothing else, you will have an instant's concentration. If you prolong it in a straight line without thinking of anything else, you will attain a concentration of some seconds. With your finger, then, trace in the air several large figures without interrupting their continuity. Follow them attentively. Make, for example, each of the figures below five times each.

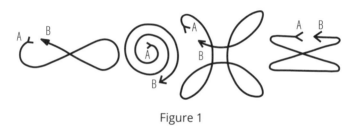

Figure 1

A student came to me one day with the complaint of great mental wandering in his study. There was no particular focus point around which his distractions would come and go. He began to do these exercises for about five minutes in the morning, again at noon, in the afternoon, and at night. In four days he could do them naturally and without distractions. He then went on to do the ones illustrated below. They are a bit more difficult and demand a more prolonged attention.

I also taught him to trace in the air giant capital letters and whole words in which there was no break in the continuity, always watching his finger with tranquil attention.

After ten days of this somewhat artificial education, he was able to leave these crutches behind and apply his attention to the book he was studying. He easily succeeded in making résumés of short paragraphs, then longer passages and even a half page at a single reading.

A businessman was on the verge of a collapse because of excessive work and the nervous tension under which he was living. He went to Dr. George W. Hall, an eminent neurologist. After the diagnosis was made that there was no acute organic lesion of any kind, he asked for a treatment which would permit him to reknit as soon as possible the rhythms of his accelerated life. Dr. Hall suggested that he have an aquarium of tropical fish built in his private office and that he spend an hour every day peacefully watching the graceful convolutions of those little creatures. The patient was a bit nonplussed, but followed the prescription faithfully. Before the year was out he sent a donation to Dr. Hall's hospital as a token of gratitude for his cure. The fish were tracing out the types of maneuvers which we here recommend.

Internal visual concentration. It will sometimes be helpful to do the same maneuvers mentally, without the aid of your hand, as if upon a blackboard. Practice this, too, for several days.

Auditory concentration. We shall explain auditory concentration in the form of an actual case. One woman found it hard to follow spoken addresses or lectures. The effort to concentrate brought on such a nervous strain that several times she had to leave the hall. And a slight noise would awaken her at night. Whether at home or in the office she could not read or write if anyone were, for instance, to move about or play a piano in her vicinity.

For several days she exercised herself in voluntarily encouraging different kinds of noises. Then she would follow the sound of a clock, saying and hearing mentally, "Tick-tock, tick-tock," about ten times with perfect concentration. On the second day she reached fifteen and on the fourth more than twenty without a thought of anything else. To this exercise she gave at most only five minutes each time. But she did it about eight times a day. Once she had satisfactorily obtained this auditory concentration, she went on to listen voluntarily to an address or lecture. At first she listened for ten, then fifteen minutes or more without fear or distractions. When these did come, her only care was to fix her attention anew on what was being said. In a month she was cured.

She also undertook to do these exercises in the midst of noise and other people's conversations. When she had no more fear of these difficulties and was no longer annoyed by the conversation of others, she could at last work peacefully and tranquilly.

Concentration in the midst of noise. We recommend this same procedure to people who have to work amidst the racket of an office, or conversations or music, where the distractions are many and fatigue is so easily induced. They should practice for only a few minutes at first. Then they should do it for a longer time till they learn to be completely independent of what is going on around them. They should imitate children who can attend to their book or lesson without bothering about the shouts of their companions. It never occurs to children to make a protest against noise. In the sincere acceptance of noise is the main part of the remedy. This is also a good way to get to sleep.

Figure 2

Touch concentration. Preserve for a few seconds the sensation of hardness, cold, heat, and the like when you touch an object.

Concentration on movement. When walking, for example, realize now that the right foot is moving, now the left, then the whole body. For this exercise you will of course have to move slowly or you will be unable to feel those sensations.

Concentration on one part of the body. Take your hand, for instance. Feel it as your own, as alive, while you hold it out before you. With a few days of practice you will after a few moments of concentration feel a slight prickling sensation in the part on which you are concentrating.

By this exercise Dr. Vittoz cured even some cases of paralysis which were of mental origin. For example, to move a paralyzed arm the patient first had to concentrate on one part of it. Then he changed the concentration from above to below, and vice versa. Finally the will could command movement again.

Concentration as a way to relax. This is the basis of the method of Professor Schultz. It is having great success in Germany. You concentrate your attention, for instance, on "My arm is heavy" and imagine that it is. This takes less than a minute. Then repeat this perhaps half a dozen times, and repeat the whole process twice or three times a day. Do it naturally, in a relaxed posture, seated or lying down, and with your eyes closed. Your arm will soon feel heavy, more speedily after some practice. And the sensation will spread to both arms and legs, producing a deep restoring rest.

Concentration to increase heat. In the same way, if you first think "My arm is heavy," then "It is hot," the blood vessels will relax and more blood will flow into the skin and, with that, greater heat. Tibetan people are said to have used such a procedure to protect themselves against excessive cold. But be careful with this exercise; do it only under an expert's guidance, for it can produce bad results if not done right.

Concentration against pain. By the same method we can stop or lessen the feeling of pain from, say, an injury. By concentrating attention on the part affected by pain, *not on the pain itself or its causes*, a voluntary wave from within will neutralize the wave of pain from the injury outside. It will keep the pain, or most of it, from coming to the nerve centers and being felt.

A More Mental Form of Re-education

Lack of interest in what we read, hear, or do, or the greater repulsion, attraction, or importance we give to what we desire or fear are the greatest enemies of concentration. Unreasonable fears or parasite ideas, worries, or uncontrolled passions cause the most distractions. The remedy lies, as indicated above, in discovering their disturbing focus point and then weakening and even destroying it. We shall explain this more at length in chapters 5 and 10.

We must arouse interest and pleasure in what we are studying or doing by considering its utility, convenience, and ease of performance. In a word, we should see it in the light and warmth of an ideal (see chapter 15).

Concentrating in reading. Fix your attention on what you are reading until you come to the first period. Rest there a few moments with conscious sensations. Read again as far as the second period and rest again, and so on until a page is completed. Repeat this exercise three times a day. This is an excellent method for re-education and is the best way to control excessive haste and anxiety to finish the reading. This haste and anxiety cause much fatigue. More concrete means for concentrating in study, in the case of healthy people as well as sick, will be found in my work *Mental Efficiency without Fatigue.*

Neuromuscular relaxation. We said before that neuromuscular tension is usually one of the causes of bad concentration, or may be produced by it. As a matter of fact, with all mental activity there is a corresponding bodily activity in nerves and muscles. Every excess or disorder in the first is accompanied by tension or fatigue in the second.

We have all observed muscular activity in external attitudes of attention. Some of these are eager movements, shortened breath, a slight bending forward of the head, stiffening of the shoulder muscles.

Sheets of paper covered with "doodles" are often found in lecture halls and meeting rooms and give us further evidence that many people get rid of excessive tension, while concentrating, by this or some other kind of kinetic liberation. This would also seem to confirm the motor theory of consciousness.

There are many nervous or tense people who easily tire themselves out if they read or study while seated. If, instead, they read or study while walking in a garden, they can keep at it much longer. This is true because there is muscular tension while they are seated. While walking, however, they can better relax their muscles, especially those used in breathing. There are also more frequent moments of receptivity or rest.

Another effect of excessive tension is a certain tendency to overactivity when we try to surpass ourselves in vivacity and effort. We then underestimate fatigue until prostration comes.

Certain drugs are sometimes prescribed which alleviate anxiety by means of their relaxing effect on the muscles.

Practice. If you notice this tension in yourself, use the following relaxing technique. Loosen well the muscles of your forehead (without wrinkling or knitting it). Then relax the muscles around your eyes (keep a tranquil gaze like that of a contemplative). Relax and loosen your mouth (tongue, jaws, and lips). Then relax the muscles of hands and feet (let them be quiet and limp and, as it were, feel the weight of gravity). Relax especially the muscles of waist and diaphragm (let your breathing be natural, deep and rhythmical).

There is a residual tension which ordinarily remains in hypertense muscles even after the rest and relaxation of sleep. The best way to eliminate this is by rhythmic exercises of the arms and legs, bending and revolving the trunk, and exercises which make the joints more flexible.

You must, however, keep in mind that this technique will have less effect if the mental causes of tension remain with us. The mental cause is either insecurity with resulting fears or worries, or an excessive spirit of competition. These cause exaggerated effort and haste and are rooted in an overestimation of oneself. As a counterbalance to such tendencies, in addition to what we shall say in the chapters on feelings (chapters 5 and 10), we here point out the tonic and calming effects of friendship or love, a reasonable ideal, and a firm religious faith together with a pure conscience.

If you have nothing to lean upon before facing the problems which each day brings, if you cannot find within yourself the equivalent of this support, you will be disturbed and tense. For the child an external support will be his mother's love. For a wife it will be her husband. For a youth it may be a faithful friend, a self-sacrificing teacher, or his spiritual director. And for the fervent believer it will be the help of God. One's own interior support or personal security will be strengthened by lending security or support to other people. Oftentimes widows triumph in life and spread security and joy as long as their children are small, yet feel sad, insecure, and troubled when these children grow up. Give to others love, help, and protection and you will increase your own security, joy, and peace.

Excessive effort and haste disappear when we purge our ideal of strange rivalries or stratagems and accommodate it to our strength and possibilities (see chapter 15). But even when you succeed in life and see your human ideal attained, there will still remain in the depths of your being a fountain of restlessness and tension. You can only remove this if, when you think about the future, you find in firm, religious faith and a pure conscience an answer which will give you peace.

A Fundamental Axiom

We said at the beginning that we cannot at the same time be both fully receptive and productive. We cannot have a clear consciousness of a sensation and at the same instant be thinking of something else. By our very thinking of this other thing we cease to have that clear consciousness. And, vice versa, in following out an idea and concentrating our attention on it, we cease to give clear attention to our sensations. In short, when the field of consciousness is wholly occupied by sensation, there is no room for other concentration, and vice versa.

One consoling conclusion is the possibility of resting and temporarily overcoming worries, sadness, phobias, and passions. On the one hand only productive power can cause fatigue. On the other hand our receptive power can bring peace and rest. We cannot at the same time be wholly receptive and productive. But with a little training we can make ourselves merely receptive even under the influence of worries and phobias. So there follows the clear possibility of acquiring this repose and mental control by means of receptivity.

A priest once confided to me that with this means alone he succeeded in dominating an instinctive fear which he had had since childhood. "I was afraid," he told me, "of cemeteries at night. So I went to one after dark. I kept my attention continually on pious thoughts or conscious sensations. Thus I succeeded in not having the feeling of fear master me even for a minute, although several times it fought hard for entrance.

"In the same way I conquered impatience in treating with a very disagreeable person. Each time his irritating words and actions provoked me to anger, I turned my attention away from them. I concentrated on observing his mental patterns, his gestures, tone of voice, or the colors of things around us. It was a kind of mental armor which kept the explosive out."

By the same simple method of having conscious sensations when an evil impulse came, a complete cure was wrought for a man tempted impulsively to wrath and suicide. A notable improvement was brought in the same way to a young man with almost unrestrainable sexual obsessions or impulses.

From Imperfect Mastery to Control

The mentally weak or sick have no true concentration when they work or study. And during the times when they should be resting, they go on thinking of their studies or business. Or they walk wrapped in worry, doubts, or sadness. Even in sleep they attain no true repose. Instead they frequently pass the time in dreams. They produce much more than they receive. This may be graphically represented as in the following figure.

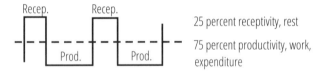

25 percent receptivity, rest

75 percent productivity, work, expenditure

Figure 3

By concentrated work at its proper time and sensations or conscious life at other times they can avoid disorder and attain the equilibrium of persons who are mentally normal. These latter, in moments of concentration or study, think only of what they are doing. They forget everything else. At other times they either have conscious sensations or think of nothing at all. In this way the time of rest or sensation is proportioned to the time of work or concentration. Their balance of activity is pictured in the following graph.

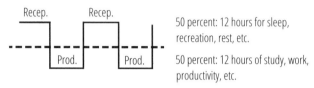

50 percent: 12 hours for sleep, recreation, rest, etc.

50 percent: 12 hours of study, work, productivity, etc.

Figure 4

Mental Control

We should attain such dominion over our faculties that we can pass swiftly from work to rest, from our interior world to the exterior, from concentration to sensation and vice versa, changing from graph A to graph B (below).

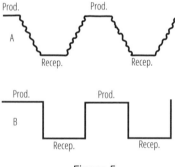

Figure 5

In graph A the shift from work to rest comes with a period of intermediate agitation, with fluctuations of work.

In graph B the transition from concentration to sensation is fast and immediate, without fluctuations or intermediate states.

To attain this control it will help to pass the hand of a clock mentally from one hour to another. Interpose conscious sensations after concentrating on each hour for a few seconds.

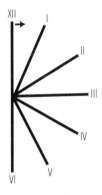

Figure 6

Do the exercise this way. Say "Twelve o'clock" and imagine the hand on XII. Concentrate your attention there. Then rest with a few sensations. Then say "One o'clock" and mentally shift the hand from XII to I. Concentrate and rest as before. Thus cover this half of the clock in one or two minutes of intermittent concentration. Do this exercise, also, three times a day.

Use these exercises to produce a healthful habit of rest, conscious life, and concentration. They directly attack mental vagueness, excess, and disorder. They must be done methodically and constantly by dedicating to them several times a day a few minutes which are free from every other occupation. *Without having put them into practice you will find it hard to understand the utility of this part of the book.* Be careful in these exercises to avoid anything which is negative or depressing. Instead of reminding us of our illness or deficiency, they should help us to forget it. They should convince us that we are controlling our illness by making us take more joy in the present and in the real world. They shall make us feel that we have more freedom and have greater mastery of ourselves. Perform them, then, with zest, as a sort of mental sport, without worry or anxiety, without attributing to them a greater efficacy than they have.

Maximum Normal Concentration Period
Fixed and clear concentration on a single sensation or idea, without repeating the impulse to pay attention to it, will only last a few seconds, scarcely half a minute. Yet you can pay attention to successive sensations or reasoning processes for a longer time. All in all, our maximum effort at concentration will normally last about twenty minutes. We do not exceed this without placing an unnecessary strain on ourselves. We must then rest for an instant and relax our attention. This is what we do instinctively when turning the page of a book or changing our position.

This is why we should interrupt our reading after fifteen or twenty minutes and take a few moments of rest by conscious sensations. Hence, also, the pedagogical necessity in lectures or sermons, especially if we are talking to children, of relaxing the audience's attention with a digression, story, or joke. If we do not grant the audience this rest they will take it for themselves and thus lose the thread of our discourse. In this as in most matters difficulties should be reasons for greater courage and energy, not excuses for sloth or cowardice. Just as a tree grows more luxuriantly beneath the pruning knife, so our spirit becomes stronger and more agile with the struggle.

OUTLINE DIAGRAM

Mental Activity and Re-education

Mental activity

Receptive

What it is	Receiving successive sensations into consciousness / A kind of passive attention
Effects	Peace, rest, tonic, joy
Re-education	Conscious sensations / Conscious acts

Productive

What it is	Producing images, reasoning processes / Active attention	
Efficient	Concentration on one idea only / Minimal "physical" fatigue / Maximum return	
Defective	Attention with distractions / Greater fatigue / Less return	
Harmful	Following several ideas at once / Harmful effects on vision / Causes	Maximum fatigue / Minimum return
Re-education	Sensual	Visual concentration / Concentration on sound and touch / Concentration on one part of the body
	Mental	Concentration in reading / Removing worries / Arousing interest
	Neuromuscular relaxation	
Fundamental axiom	You do not produce and receive simultaneously so learn to rest and control yourself	
From imperfect mastery to control	Equilibrium through rapid transition from concentration to sensation	
Maximum concentration period		

4

Acts of the Will

"I will" is a phrase rarely meant though much in use. A man
who comes to realize the secret of really using his will, though
today he be poor and lonely, will soon surpass all others.

—Lacordaire

Definition

The will is a rational appetite which tends toward the good,
once the good is apprehended by our intellect. It is also the
executive power of our personality by which we choose and
pursue definite goals and the means to those goals. Accommodated to mental treatment, the will may be described as
an individual energy by which we are able freely to organize
the representation of an act and freely to determine its execution. The greatest of our mental energies, it will, if well
channeled, most quickly cure us. This energy is accumulated
in deliberation and discharged in decision. It is distinct from
our acts. It is free, active, and guided by intelligence. Even in
the case of people with nervous and emotional disturbances
and conflicts, even in cases of apparent loss of willpower, this
energy still exists, though latent and unused.

False or Ineffective Acts of the Will

Ineffectual desire: passive, necessary; the presentation of a good object suffices for our will to desire it.

Vague intention, or "having a mind" to do something: this is a kind of tendency to do something; it is not even wanting it, but a vague plan or attempt to want it.

Impulse: this is being determined by external circumstances or forces; it is indeliberate, instinctive, a great force but a chaotic one.

Velleity: this is an absence of the feeling of personality; "I would like to," but not "I will."

Effective Acts of the Will

Those acts truly and fully come from our will which leave us with the persuasion and intimate conviction that they are free.

This kind of act truly educates the will. It leads most quickly to a cure. Its source is willpower. This is the "deliberate determination" of which St. Ignatius Loyola, founder of the Society of Jesus, speaks in his book, *The Spiritual Exercises*.

Theory of Dr. Vittoz

This theory, not yet substantiated, bases its description of this act of will upon what he claimed he was able to feel when placing his hand lightly on a patient's forehead.

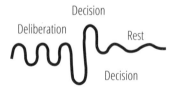

Figure 7

First he felt the pulsations, as he says, which reflect deliberation. They are similar to those of perfect concentration. Then there are one or several stronger waves which correspond to decision or discharge of the will. Finally there is the smooth rhythm of repose.

Dr. Vittoz and his students, by their refined sense of touch, perceived "brain pulsations" which they distinguished from the ordinary pulse. These they found useful for the external observation and control of a patient's mental acts.

Their distinction and classification, done "grosso modo" by the Lausanne school, confirms and synthesizes what has been explained above.

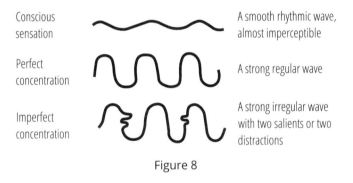

Figure 8

Note that these graphic representations of the waves give us, in their general pattern, the immediate impression that conscious sensations are a tonic activity of our mental system and produce rest.

Secondly, note that defective "production," or simultaneous work at several ideas, disturbs, fatigues, and weakens us.

Finally, as pictured in the will curve, decision produces peace and rest. Indecision, on the contrary, is a source of fatigue. For the brain then overloads itself with energies which find no outlet.

Requisites for True Acts of the Will

1. *Make the act concrete.* Picture clearly to yourself what you are going to do. Concentrate your attention on this image. The more detailed and vivid an image you form, the more force it will have. Lack of this requisite is a prime source of lack of willpower in people with emotional or nervous disturbances. It is hard for them to halt the flow of their ideas. Their productive power does not obey them thoroughly. They find it hard to concentrate on what they are going to do.

To concentrate well on what you plan to do, answer the following questions: "What am I going to do? When must it be done? How?" Consider also the other conditions necessary for execution. Our most noble faculty is not put in motion when it does not know where it is going. Because of this lack of precision many pretended plans do not pass from the stage of desire, or velleity, or incipient intention. There is no mental discharge in them. Here we have the main cause of inefficiency in what we thought were decisions. They were too vague, not concrete.

2. *Feel the possibility of execution.* The queen of our faculties is too conscious of its dignity to throw itself consciously into a frustration. It will not exert a force which it knows must be sterile. Once the act is made concrete, examine yourself to see whether the energy you possess is equal to the energy necessary for the act. You should feel this possibility somewhat as an athlete feels whether he has the needed muscular strength to perform some feat.

3. *Have a motive.* Our will is an energy ruled by intelligence and naturally inclined toward the good. You should perceive values, goods, motives for an act. To obtain strength of will these motives should be:

> *Objective*: good in themselves, not merely because of other considerations.

> *Subjective*: perceived as good by you.

> *Charged with emotion*: the good is not only perceived on an intellectual level, but is heartfelt also. It interests one's whole being.

> *Accommodated* to your individual capacity. This will be more the motive of a sense of good for the young, more the motive of abstract goodness for adults.

> *Actuated* or *remembered*: either put into action at the very moment of decision, or stored up for the moment decided upon for execution.

4. *Make a sincere will act or decision.* This is the condition most frequently absent and causing most failures of will. It consists in really determining yourself. Decision converts a plan to present or future reality. Decision makes a real actuality of what is merely possible. By decision you give the victory to a practical idea by excluding the opposite or alternatives as if impossible for you. By this sincerity you *feel* that the "Yes" or "No" is true, effective, certain. You are left with the conviction that the object of your act of will must be realized and that its existence is already assured. The deep-rooted cause of our weakness and impotency is in the slackness of our willing. When something is really

willed, then hitherto unsuspected energies are released even by weak organisms.

Execution

Decision introduces a great force into consciousness which carries it naturally onward toward act. If you can perform the act immediately, then this force is discharged without a new intervention of consciousness. If the execution is for some future time, the order will be transmitted and reserves of energy will remain on the subconscious level. They will be ready to work automatically at the proper time unless you intervene with a counter-order or some unforeseen obstacle occurs.

For example, I decide to go visit a friend after dinner. As a matter of fact I take my hat, board the streetcar, and ride until I arrive at his house without making a new conscious act.

There are people who decide to rise at a determined time, and then the subconscious which never sleeps arouses them at the exact hour. It will even do this before the hour if they are worried about it.

Once you have decided that you must accept a certain practical idea, and have excluded the opposite as impossible, never discuss it at the time of execution. This would equivalently annihilate the decision. Instead, do it blindly. Suppose you decide to arise at the first sound of the alarm clock. On hearing it, never stop to argue the matter. Do not stop to think whether or not you are still tired or whether it is still early. But immediately jump out of bed.

If the execution costs you some trouble or is repugnant to your instincts, as in making a necessary apology, in the time intervening between decision and execution do not even think about what you are going to do. For then the instinctive objections would reappear. At most, think only of the good consequences which your understanding foresees.

If your decision is to avoid an action to which you are attracted by instinct (some illicit pleasure, for instance), it will be better not to think of it at all. Every idea tends toward the act. If perchance you *must* think of it, then let it not be a concrete idea. An idea is more compelling the more concrete it is and the stronger impression it makes on you. Consider only the repulsive aspect of the act and its occasions, or its harmful consequences.

This is a means to perform easily acts which are subjectively heroic. Decide upon the act in the light and warmth of some principal motive. Then for the interval preceding its execution do not think about the act or the contrary motives which unconscious repugnance will present. In short, *you should not think about an act for a longer time than you need to reach a decision.* And when the moment comes, execute it blindly as if it were something automatic which it were impossible not to do. When you decide upon a supernatural act, such as practice of virtue, you need God's supernatural help. Remember that this will never be denied you if you ask for it with trust and humility.

To make the most effective use of the will, the queen of our faculties, we should accustom ourselves to follow this procedure. On feeling an impulse to do this or that, we should always leave an interval between it and carrying out the impulse. This is allowing time for deliberation. It is the same as saying, "Look before you leap." Before the act of will itself we should ask ourselves, "Shall I actually will this [something concrete]? For what motives?" In the decision itself we should answer, "I do really will it," or "It will be done." We make a firm and concrete act of the will and buttress it by feeling its possibility, usefulness, and even necessity. Then we should finally clinch the matter by excluding even the thought of an opposite decision, insisting with ourselves, "It's all settled. Now we go into action."

OUTLINE DIAGRAM

Acts of the Will

Definition	Tendency toward the good Our executive power Energy that is free, active, guided by intelligence		
Will acts	False will acts	Mere desire Vague intention Instinctive impulse Velleity ("I would like to")	
	Aspects of true will acts	Mental	Concrete object Possibility felt to be so Motive Sincere decision
Re-education	Feel your act of will progress from external to internal acts Decide the means to take		
Execution	Immediate		
	Long term	Do not discuss the plan decided Do not even think about it till the time comes	

5

Feelings and Emotions

Although intellectual error brings many to the precipice of evil and disgrace, wanton feelings and emotions are responsible for many more physical tragedies.

External and internal sense experiences affect the sensible part of our organism. Merely speculative ideas or images affect the understanding; decisions affect the will. Many of these are only partial reactions of our human system and pass, without other consequences, into the archives of our memory. But there are certain other experiences, ideas, and memories with an affective charge of fear or hope, joy or sadness, hatred, wrath, love, etc.; and these affect our whole being. They do not pass away so readily. Their residue tends to become encrusted in our body and keeps influencing the higher levels of personality. Certain feelings and emotions resonate in our nervous system and our whole being, in one way at the presence of happiness, in another way at its absence. Real or imaginary success, for instance, is accompanied by positive emotions. Negative emotions accompany failure or disgrace.

Pleasant feelings help to preserve our normal physiological rhythms. But in emergency situations emotions arise which modify these rhythms, activate our muscular system, and stimulate hormonal production. This total resonance—in the activation of our nervous, muscular, and hormonal systems —is necessary for normal development and the balanced functioning of our organism and our spirit. So, for instance, if a child grows up without enough love, security, and joy, he will become defective or abnormal. When there is an emotional deficiency in childhood, often the youth or adult turns out to be a social misfit, even as infant malnutrition is related to later proclivity to tuberculosis. The emotionally starved child in some cases later turns out to have a cold and calculating temperament, incapable of affection. Another will have an exaggerated tendency to hatred, suspicion, and sadness. Another will be timid, self-belittling, indecisive, or a frustrated pessimist. As the remedy for malnutrition is a fortified diet, so the remedy for emotional starvation includes a prolonged injection of positive emotions.

On the other hand, excessively prolonged or intensified *negative* emotions, such as wrath, fear, and sadness, can leave the spirit and body of a man conditioned or inclined toward disgust, insecurity, and frustration. And this is especially true when he had to suffer such negative experiences as a child, with body and soul unprepared for them.

There is an intricate labyrinth of definitions and theories about feelings or emotions, their species, causes, and effects. But the main point of interest in a practical manual such as this is to know their influence on mental fatigue, weakness, and psychosomatic diseases, and to point out some norms for channeling and governing them.

Emotional Mechanism:
The Psycho-physiological Trajectory of an Emotion

Any event may be the occasion of emotions: the sight of a lightning bolt or a savage animal, a lion's roar or the crash of thunder, insults from an enemy, the death of a dear one, a sudden pain, news that surgery is needed, business or academic failure, or even a vivid memory of a great past danger or humiliation.

By the pathways of the senses or imagination these stimuli reach the cerebral cortex. Then my reason, if I am alert, will analyze and interpret them peacefully, and relate them to my happiness without giving room to a frantic imagination to go to work on them. But if I perceive, or think I perceive, in them something contrary to my happiness — or the symbols of happiness such as life, health, comfort, wealth, honor, personal caprice, or my ideals — then my cerebral cortex will send to the hypothalamus, down in my middle brain, an alarm or emergency call asking for the tremendous force of the emotions to be released for defense of my happiness. And emotional force is unleashed on the instant.

The *occasion* of our wrath or fear is the event. But the real cause is in the "Ego," in the interpretation we give to the event, using either our reason or imagination, and connecting the event with our own personal happiness. If we see in the event an obstacle which we can remove or destroy, we react by anger. If we see it as a danger or mighty opposing force which we cannot overcome, our reaction is fear. If the event means our own failure or some loss, we grow sad. The emotion itself is produced, consciously or unconsciously, by an idea or mental image. In brief, an angry reaction may be summarized in these key words: "I, He, It." "I who am so good, so wise … I cannot tolerate such treatment. My status and wishes should be respected." Or, "He or They … are unjust, cruel, discourteous … and should be reprimanded." Or, "It (the event) is intolerable." In fear, the content of the emotion will be, for instance, "A great harm or danger is hovering over me; it is unavoidable." And in sadness and depression, "My loss is total and irreparable."

Organic effects. Any of these thoughts, or a memory or vivid image of them is like an alarm signal which goes to the hypothalamus in the middle brain to summon our emotional energy to protect our happiness. The hypothalamus is, as it were, the "control room" of our emotional machinery. It responds instantaneously, sets up the vegetative nervous system for struggle, immediately tenses the muscles (a battle attitude), and, if the emotion is intense, also puts our internal secretion glands into a state of hyperactivity. Such tension, if intense or repeated, may affect the whole organism or its weakest parts and produce functional disorders and pains which are called psychosomatic: somatic because they affect the body (soma); psychical because they are produced by ideas and feelings in the psyche (in the "spirit").

If the tension is localized in the blood vessels, we grow pale because they contract (as in fear). Other emotions dilate the blood vessels and then the skin flushes and turns red. It is thought that 80 percent of headaches are caused by tension that is emotionally produced in the neck muscles.

The anxious effort to see or read better or faster produces other tensions in the muscles which accommodate the eye to vision, and finally causes hypermetropia or functional defective vision.

OUTLINE DIAGRAM

Emotional Machinery

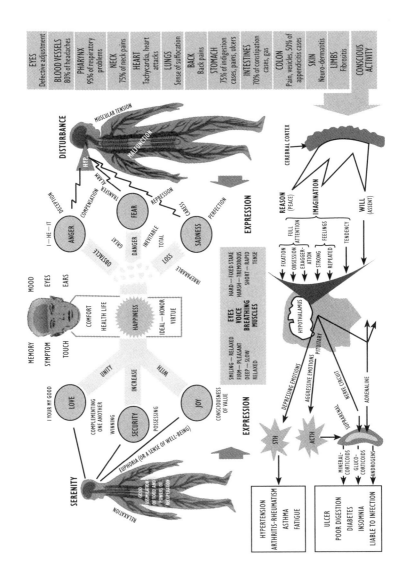

When tension is connected with the lungs, we experience a feeling of suffocation or hyperventilation, and even dizziness or nausea, for we are then losing carbon dioxide and not getting enough oxygen. Regarding the heart, most instances of tachycardia, or strong palpitations, have an emotional source.

After the heart and lungs the digestive tract is most frequently affected by the emotions. A study made at Massachusetts General Hospital showed the following: 96 percent of the colitis cases were nourishing feelings of resentment; 75 percent suffered from feelings of discouragement; 68 percent were being tortured by remorse. The bitter wave of hatred or sadness was overflowing into their intestines. Half of the diabetic and cardiopathic cases examined were influenced by emotions either causing or accompanying them. And many cases of arterial hypertension, with no trace of an organic cause, were improved by improving the patient's mental attitudes.

Bad news or a bad mood often result in loss of appetite, indigestion, or nausea. Such renowned institutions as the Mayo Clinic and the Oschner Clinic attribute 74 to 75 percent of their gastrointestinal cases to an emotional origin.

Seventy percent of cases of constipation are attributed to sadness or disgust, and many cases of diarrhea are due to fear or anxiety. Just one case in point: that of the widow who suffered from severe constipation while her two sons were away from home at a boarding school, but was perfectly normal whenever her boys were living at home.

Prolonged tension can produce pain: an ulcer-like pain in the stomach, an appendicitis-like pain in the upper colon, other pains in the lower colon. Fifty percent of these cases are found to have an emotional cause.

One young man complained of appendicitis, but an X-ray examination revealed only that it seemed to be normal. The man insisted, "I don't want to keep something that has caused me such pain. Cut it out." He was operated on with partial anesthesia so that he would feel no pain, but was thoroughly conscious. The surgeon noticed signs of previous tension in the colon close to the appendix and thought to himself that this was the cause of the pain, probably emotional in origin. He asked the patient, "Have you any problem with the law? The police are at the door to see you." At that the surgeon could see the man's colon tightening at the place where signs of previous tension remained. The man was an ex-convict. When he heard that the police were looking for him, the thought of danger alarmed him and this showed up in the weak portion of his colon.

None of all this means that such pains or troubles are unreal or purely due to the patient's imagination. They are real physical illnesses. A doctor will examine the patient and perhaps make a diagnosis that there is nothing wrong. This means that the organs are completely healthy, but their functioning is disturbed by some emotion. Such a functional illness, if uncorrected, can in the progress of time affect the organ itself.

Repeated tension related to the skin causes many cases of neurodermatitis, and in the limbs muscular rheumatism or fibrositis. And the richer our affective endowment and clearer our intelligence, the more exposed we are to such illnesses if we do not control ourselves. For we shall be able to see a dozen points worth our active concern where those less endowed would see only one, and we shall also be inclined to take upon ourselves many more responsibilities.

We may call this whole process the spontaneous and simple muscular phase of an emotion. It develops within fractions of a second without time for deliberation, and so there can be in it no question of moral responsibility or sin. We call this phase "muscular" because its effects can be explained by muscular reaction without much hormonal intervention. We call it "simple" to distinguish it from other kinds of excitation which are stronger and which at once summon into action the full force of hormonal activity.[5]

The More Conscious and Reinforced Emotion ("Hormonal Phase")

In this phase, organic commotion reaches and affects the cerebral cortex. We become aware that our muscles are preparing for attack or defense. Sometimes the stimulus itself, or the memory of it, persists. There may be, then, three reactions: from the reason, the imagination, or the will.

1. We may allow our *reason* to think peacefully about the event and the accompanying bodily commotion. On discovering that the latter is really unnecessary and the event not really disastrous and that it may involve other good and greater effects, the disturbance settles down and peace returns. But too often, unfortunately, we give rein to the imagination instead.

2. The imagination peremptorily demands that *full attention* be given to its fears, disgust, or sadness. It is then very difficult to concentrate on anything else whatsoever. Recall, for instance, what happens in a moment of wrath. If anyone

---

[5] We make this distinction for the sake of pedagogical clarity. In practice these phases nearly always go together.

comes to speak to us about another matter, we can scarcely pay attention to what he is saying. The same thing happens if we are seriously worried. Then it is very difficult to pay attention to the content of a reading or conference. The emotional force demands that full attention be paid to itself. And such full attention easily terminates in a complete blocking of the mind in one of the following forms:

a. *An obsession.* A sexual thought or a thought of a present or imminent disaster will not leave us in peace for a moment, unless we busy ourselves with something extremely interesting. It struggles continually to occupy the center of our attention. A scruple is no more than an obsession of fear. The way to conquer it is by giving less importance to the imaginary eternal loss, convincing ourselves that it is an emotional illness which cannot have eternal consequences and by diverting our attention from the thought which produces the emotion. So we shall refuse to follow that train of thought even for the sake of removing the doubt, in practice treating the thought with disdain.

b. *A fixation.* Unpleasant impressions or thoughts tend to *engrave themselves and become fixed* in our minds by repetition unless we succeed in forgetting or ignoring them. They will be engraved even deeper if we give them importance and fear them. A case in point would be that of the person who struggles against impure thoughts in a spirit of fear. They would gradually disappear if he despised them (instead of fearing them) and, in practice, went on as if he did not have them. Worry is a fine thread of fear which traces a path across the life of our spirit. Unless we succeed in breaking it early, while it is still weak, it will open up into a deep crevasse into which all our attention and thoughts will be channeled.

c. *Exaggeration.* The ills or dangers that beset us will almost always tend to be exaggerated. If we surrender to this tendency to exaggerate, we shall end up terrified or infuriated by trivialities. If we have caught ourselves in this type of exaggeration, we should learn a lesson to apply to our whole life: "I see that I have a personal tendency to exaggerate and I dread a hundred dangers where there is only one. Therefore, whenever I catch myself worrying a lot in advance, I shall react with a deliberately chosen attitude of joy and smiling peace, because I know that the reason for fear is insignificant."

d. *Transfer.* Finally we can transfer the emotion from its true cause to one of its concomitant circumstances, as in the case of conditioned reflexes. Take, for example, the case of a child who was hurt and frightened at receiving an injection from a nurse dressed in white, and afterward is frightened by anything colored white. How important for him to discover early the cause of this false transference!

By interpreting the stimulus, the imagination can strengthen and repeat the negative feelings of sadness or fear. And such a repetition is, as we hinted earlier, the principal cause of very many psychosomatic illnesses. Such an illness can at times be incurred by a single, very strong experience, a psychical trauma. One man, for instance, started across the railroad tracks without noticing that an electric train was coming. The train passed so close to him that it almost grazed him. His emotional reaction was so strong that he fainted dead away before he took a dozen steps further. At the hospital they found so much sugar in his blood that they treated him as a diabetic. But when he regained consciousness, he assured them he had never been a diabetic, and told them the story of what happened.

Most frequently such emotional illnesses come about as the result of *minor* emotions which are, however, repeated often. The following case will be an illustration from animal psychology. Electric wires are attached to the feet of sheep and, while they are grazing peacefully, enough current is sent through for them to feel it. The animals tremble for a moment, the current is interrupted, and they go on feeding in peace. Every five minutes this experience is repeated, for weeks on end, without their organisms becoming in the least abnormal. Then an emotional element is introduced into the experience. A bell is rung ten seconds before the current is turned on. The sheep soon relate the sound of the bell with the unpleasantness of the electric shock. As soon as they hear the bell, they stop grazing and go into a state of painful anticipation. When this experience is repeated every five minutes for several days, the animals stop eating altogether, will not even stand up on their feet, and finally go into a labored breathing which signals death. And so the experiment had to be stopped.

How much emotional rest does an organism need in order to keep off death? Or how long a time should pleasant emotions last in order to counter the effect of unpleasant emotions?

When the sheep were given two to four hours of pleasant experiences in a fine pasture, they resisted perfectly the impact of the unpleasant emotions for the rest of the day. This is not unlike the case of human beings. If we make of family life a haven of love, the negative emotions we may experience in office or factory will be counteracted. If we have a sincere spiritual life, in it we shall find the best counterweight to daily dissatisfactions and fears. If in prayer we take account of the fact that we are having an interview with Infinite Wisdom, Goodness, and Power, this will give us a great degree of satisfaction. And if, in the performance of our duties, we understand that we are fulfilling the will of God—that is, the ideal of Infinite Wisdom or, in other words, that we are doing the noblest and most useful task that anyone could accomplish in the circumstances—we can have hours of emotional fullness to immunize us against many psychosomatic illnesses.

The third effect of an emotional exaggeration upon our imagination is oftentimes to leave engraved in the subconscious a *permanent feeling or tendency.* So much so that the dividing line tends to disappear between a repeated feeling and a permanent tendency to insecurity, sadness, or disgust. The victim of such a tendency feels happy as long as he is kept busy. But as soon as his mind is unoccupied, thoughts of insecurity and sadness enter in, and these rob him of all peace and satisfaction.

The formation of such a tendency, e.g., of insecurity, is not due so much to the actual terror or failure as to *a negative manner of reacting to it.* After the event there would be nothing or almost nothing remaining behind in the subconscious if only one were convinced, either by his own efforts or those of his educators or advisers, that there was no such great reason for fear. But if these startling experiences are not balanced by more mature thought, a kind of sediment of insecurity will remain behind after they have passed. And this insecurity will be all the greater depending upon the intensity and frequency of acts, feelings, or imagination of terror produced by horror movies, for instance, or horror stories told to children at nighttime. Such a tendency, mixed with exaggeration, or transference, can produce a lasting disequilibrium, a neurosis. This, as a kind of intruder sun, will disturb one's whole psychical system.

Neurosis. Out internal world may be compared to a planetary system. Around the will, or rational power of appetite, the queen of our faculties, there should gravitate all our psychical life: our sensations, impressions, ideas, reasoning, and deliberate will acts. As in a planetary system, when the sun exerts its influence upon the planets, order reigns and equilibrium, so also in ourselves, when the whole life of our spirit, our psychical life, is obedient to our will. However, if an intruder sun were to insert itself within the orbit of solar attraction and, instead of being subject to the sun, were instead to exercise its own attraction upon the other stars or planets, there would arise disequilibrium and disorder in proportion as it remained independent of the sun and as its own powers of attraction were more intense.

In our interior world this intruder sun would be the strong emotion, not countered or transferred, which takes over within us. Sometimes this would be due to phobia or groundless fear which we cannot master, or a scruple or worry which pursues us incessantly, or a seemingly irresistible attraction or impulse. Such phenomena keep on attracting to themselves other thoughts, acts, feelings. The longer they last, the more satellites they will have, and the weaker and more disturbed will be the will's field of action. To weaken their influence we must remove their satellites. That is, we should not think or act deliberately while under their influence. Most of all, we should find out how they first appeared on the scene within us and how to destroy them.

3. *The third reaction* possible is for the free will to accept the imagination's interpretation of the stimulus, and even assist it by ordering one's actions accordingly, like the scrupulous person who keeps confessing the same thing over and over again, despite having been forbidden to do so by his director. Or like the man who consents to hatred and attacks his enemy.

With such frequent and intense irrational reactions in the cerebral cortex, the new stimulation of the hypothalamus will be all the stronger. And if this, at the first signal of alarm, already responds by putting the entire autonomous nervous system in a state of struggle for its own happiness, now it will also throw into action the immense force of the internal secretion glands. The alarm is passed on to the neighboring pituitary gland which directly or indirectly controls the organism's internal hormonal functions. The pituitary gland produces or controls the distribution of a dozen important hormones. Here we are particularly interested in two of them: the adrenocorticotropic hormone (ACTH) and the somatotropic hormone (HGH).

Depressive emotions and STH. When destructive external agents such as poison, infection, heat, or cold invade the organism, the pituitary gland liberates a great quantity of STH to prepare the organism against the invader by providing antibodies, heat, inflammation, etc. The same thing happens when we run into depressing situations or emotions such as sadness, frustration, despair, discouragement, and indecision. This excess of STH can produce hypertension, arthritis, asthma, fatigue, and so on. At the Catholic University of Montreal, Dr. Selye kept injecting STH into animals for a period of time and then submitting them to large dosages of salt; he produced hypertension in them. When, instead of giving them salt, he applied cold and moisture to their joints, rheumatoid arthritis appeared. On the other hand, they contracted asthma when he made them inhale a light irritant into their bronchial tubes.

As regards fatigue, we have all had the experience that we tire very soon if we work with an attitude of discouragement, sadness, or reluctance or, what comes to the same thing, with an excess of STH. On the other hand, we scarcely feel fatigue when we have enthusiasm, joy, and optimism. For instance, a mother feels little fatigue when she is working and watching her beloved child.

Aggressive emotions and ACTH. At times our emotions are not the kind that wear us down or depress us, but rather aggressive emotions, such as wrath or resentment. Or we fall into the attitude of the eternal reformer, discontent with everything and everybody. Or the idealist or perfectionist who sets a goal beyond his real possibilities and lives in a state of urgency, haste, and dissatisfaction; or the overly ambitious person who is driven to overactivity by an uncontrolled sense of competition.

In such instances the pituitary gland liberates the hormone ACTH, which does not spread throughout the whole body like

STH, but goes to the cortex of the suprarenal glands (above the kidneys) and stimulates them into activity. Here is the principal factory of the hormones which are organic "bombs." They are tiny molecules, but have a great effect on our health or sickness. In the external part of the suprarenal glands, twenty-seven important hormones are produced, among them the well-known cortisone. In the medulla (the internal part) of the suprarenal glands adrenaline is produced. This is a hormone which swiftly gives the organism a great amount of energy for fleeing danger or reaching out to attain happiness. The daily newspapers often supply us with such examples as that of the young mother, a slightly built woman, who was able all by herself to lift the rear end of a heavy automobile from her child. In ordinary circumstances she would have been completely unable to summon such an output of energy.

Here we must needs admire the wisdom of the Creator who arranged that adrenaline would not be produced in the cortex or as an effect of ACTH like the twenty-seven other hormones, for then its saving action would be likely to take effect when it was too late. In such a case (1) the hypothalamus would have to get the alarm signal. Then (2) this would stimulate the pituitary gland. This would then (3) have to liberate ACTH into the bloodstream. (4) Little by little the blood would carry ACTH to the suprarenal glands. And (5) only then would adrenaline be spread throughout the organism to produce the force and strength required. In such a case, we would not have the extraordinary emergency strength needed at that precise emotional moment and would be unable to flee or attack effectively.

But God has so arranged it that adrenaline will not arrive too late. Adrenaline is elaborated in the medulla of the suprarenal glands which is directly connected with the hypothalamus by means of the nervous system. As a result, when the hypothalamus receives the alarm signal, adrenaline is released within fractions of a second.

If these twenty-eight activation hormones are present in *excessive* amounts as a result of repeated or exaggerated emotions, it is evident that they will disturb its workings and bring on illnesses. Among other distressing effects, they help to produce ulcers, diabetes, hypertension, and insomnia and make us more liable to infection. All this has been demonstrated by Dr. Selye. There follows a summary of some of his experiments.

First, Dr. Selye found that by injecting ACTH, subjecting them to irritating noises, he produced ulcers in rats. Then, to demonstrate emotional malnutrition in man, he conducted a series of experiments at the University of Montreal. He took two groups of children, one group enjoying a happy family life, the other living in unhappy or broken homes. He saw to it that both groups had the best diet, and frequently examined the functioning of their pituitary glands. He always found an excess of ACTH present in the children who lived in families characterized by terrorism, anger, and disgust. Despite their excellent diet, none of these children came up to the normal weight. On the other hand, the children leading a happy family life gained weight and enjoyed robust health.

Our pulse rate at moments of excitement or anger is found to be 170 to 200 or more beats per minute. The blood pressure rises correspondingly from 13 to 23 centimeters or more. A heart attack or a stroke is then possible, and daily experience teaches us that many people with weak hearts or circulatory systems die from these attacks when they are undergoing a period of strong emotions.

We shall consider emotionally caused insomnia and its remedy in the chapter on "Rest" (chapter 7).

Note, again, that all these illnesses are real and not a fiction of the sick person's imagination, even when the illnesses are induced or increased by the emotions. And we should also note that the richer a man's intellectual life and the nobler and readier his fellow-feelings, the greater probability there may be that he will fall into such illnesses. For the higher our aspirations and the keener our intelligence, the more difficulties we can see and the more distressed we may tend to be in comparison to others less gifted.

Control of the Emotions

To control the emotions and avoid such illnesses and unhappiness we propose the following five means:

1. Do not give room to the thought which causes the emotion. Instead, occupy your mind with another matter.
2. By education (or self-education) change your evaluation of the stimulus and become accustomed to considering the stimulus from another viewpoint.
3. Discover and modify the disturbing idea.
4. Change the negative feeling and tendency.
5. Change the expression of it to the extent that it is under your control.

1. *Do not give room to the disturbing idea.*
A. *By avoiding the occasion* of it, you can more easily avoid the thought itself which is aroused on such and such an occasion.

This course of action is often possible. And in some matters it is necessary and obligatory; for instance, in cases of sexual excitation. Moral theologians teach us that even to put oneself in such an occasion without necessity is sinful and presumptuous. Since this is such a slippery terrain, if we so much as enter upon it we are liable to fall.

B. *Occupy your whole attention with other matters.*
1. *By fully conscious sensations* (chapter 3). Recall the case of the young man with a compulsive tendency to suicide. He gained control and was cured by interposing conscious sensations whenever he experienced that impulse.
2. *Avoid the thought which arouses the emotion by busying yourself with attractive occupations or pastimes.* Have a hobby or harmless amusement to resort to in moments of depression, fatigue, or a negative emotion. The collector who loses himself for a while in his collections. Or the artist with his music or painting, and the gardener with his flowers.
3. *Pay better attention to what you are doing or saying* rather than to the subjective thoughts which disturb you; for instance, if you blush or tremble before a public appearance. That is how I myself conquered a childhood fear of cemeteries at night. I deliberately went there alone and spent some time praying for the repose of the souls of those who were buried there. The devotional attitude took up my attention, and so my fearful imagination could not control my mind.

And is not this the way that mothers everywhere handle the emotions of their babies? When the infant cries in fear, anger, or sadness, the mother shows it something new and, by distracting its attention, succeeds in interrupting or allaying the childish emotion.

2. Change your evaluation of the stimulus.
The stimulus is connected with a sorrow, humiliation, failure, offense, and so forth. Your course of action is to weigh carefully just what good elements there are in such an event. Then you will have pleasant thoughts instead of those which are sad, depressing, or frustrating. And if these cross our minds we can control them by the opposite pleasant thoughts. This is not the work of a day, but the result of an education in magnanimity, goodness, understanding, faith, and fortitude. Some of the ancient philosophers of Greece and Rome attained this to a high degree guided only by the light of natural reason. They insisted that we must accept suffering as a help to be stronger and more understanding and patient with others.

However, in the most difficult and bitter crises of life it is scarcely possible for merely philosophical considerations to bring us equanimity and joy. For sorrow, humiliation, failure, sickness, and death seem meaningless when we separate them from considerations of God and eternity. At such moments only religion offers us a peaceful point of view. Then if we look upon ourselves as pilgrims in this world, moving in the direction of our eternally happy homeland, it is possible to depreciate a passing sorrow. And if we meditate upon what Holy Scripture says about a passing tribulation producing for us "an eternal weight of glory," we can even begin to rejoice at suffering.

A deeply religious education makes such a solution easier. Such an educational background will include as a model an Infinite God who deliberately chose suffering and humiliation for Himself, for His Mother and His Apostles. Only in the light of eternity can we make light of temporal afflictions. And we can accept human suffering and humiliations in the light of the divine honor and joy which we expect to receive in return for them. We can come to love such sufferings or humiliations only if we imitate the saints and look upon them as the caresses, embraces, love, and mercy of our Heavenly Father and signs of divine predilection.

In the chapters of Part 2 we shall explain the concrete methods by which we can overcome thoughts which cause wrath, fear, and sadness.

3. *Discover and change the disturbing idea.*
Modify: (a) its content, (b) the reason for it, (c) its intensity and duration.

a. *Modify its content.* When the cause is conscious and concrete, it is easy to discover where it is exaggerated or illogical, and so it is easier to modify it. But sometimes we unconsciously suppress it because we do not wish inadmissible acts or motives to appear even in our minds. At other times we transfer it to other stimuli or concomitant causes. In such instances consultation with a specialist is indicated. A subconscious anxiety or disturbance in your feelings can be normalized or diminished when the idea producing it is made conscious. Hence it follows that many emotional conflicts are cured once they are made manifest and examined minutely. A detailed examination of the content of feelings and their causes and discovering the conditioned reflex in many phobias or the transference which produced them can often weaken or even do away with them. The account of conscience or report to one's personal spiritual director—practiced by many persons who are serious about progress in their spiritual life—often produces the same beneficial result.

b. *Modify the reason for it.* The reason for a feeling which may now seem illogical but which, nevertheless, we cannot now control can often be made clear if we rediscover some forgotten circumstance or repressed tendency originally associated with it. Psychiatric evaluation or certain psychological tests (the TAT,[6] for instance) can help discover it and set one free of its harmful effects.

A case in point: J. B. experienced a feeling of asphyxiation or difficulty in breathing whenever he entered a theater or a church and, to avoid this, always had to sit near a door. Was this feeling linked up with an idea of being shut in? He did not know. But when he was helped to recall the first time that he experienced this, a serious illness that befell him in a closed room, he experienced lasting relief.

c. *The intensity or emotional force* of an idea depends upon three factors.

1. *Its quality.* The more concretely an idea is represented, the more immediate force it has. The more
spiritual or abstract it is, the less emotional, but
more enduring, motive force. That is why orators

---

[6] The Thematic Apperception Test, developed at Harvard University in the 1930s, is the one of the more widely used personality tests. A patient is shown ambiguous pictures and asked to imagine and describe what is happening in the scene, what the people were doing before the scene, and so forth.

speak to the imagination to obtain an immediate
result, a feeling. But when they want a lasting effect, they try to convince the understanding.

2. *Its quantity.* The force of an idea is greater in proportion to its closer association with other ideas,
experiences, or feelings, and to the degree to which
they are more striking.

3. *Its duration.* A passing emotion, fear, or sadness
leaves little trace in the organism or mental background. But if it remains too long it can modify
them to a notable extent. It can attract into its orbit
(as we said of the intruder sun) more and more
thoughts and acts, and cause lasting disorder.

In several parts of South America I witnessed the following custom, a very pious one, if you will, but not very
Christian. And it is by no means in accordance with mental
hygiene. Women there will remain in mourning for months
and months without going out of the house or admitting
any distractions. When the period of mourning is over,
many of them have become nervous cases. Because it per-
sisted, the depressing atmosphere of mourning destroyed
their control.

Take the idea then that is bothering you and strip it of
its sensible counterpart, its importance and concrete details.
Break the links it has with other phenomena of your experience. Do not consciously dwell on it, but, as mentioned
heretofore, substitute for it a contrary thought and feeling or
at least a different one. In making this substitution, search for
other ideas which appeal to the senses as much as possible.
Symbols will have a strong appeal to your (or the patient's)
imagination. Associate these ideas with important living

realities. Repeatedly pass them through your mental field of consciousness that, like a snowball, they may gather round them as large a number of mental elements as possible.

4. *Change the negative feeling and tendency to the opposite.*
Sometimes we do succeed in changing *the idea*, but still experience an inclination toward the scruple, worry, sadness, discontent, or fear. This means that the negative *feeling* is still rooted in the subconscious and tends to bother the mind with negative thoughts. If we do not keep our mind well occupied, we shall find it possessed by sad memories, worries, disgust, and fears which are allied to that latent feeling or tendency.

The indirect remedy consists in giving no room to these thoughts, always keeping the mind busy until the tendency to sadness or fear atrophies from disuse.

The direct remedy is to change the latent tendency or, better, to implant the opposite one. Understanding how such a tendency is formed will instruct us how to fight this battle. The tendency to fear, for instance, as we have indicated above, comes about as a consequence of vivid experiences of fear which are not countered by vivid experiences of security. So, then, a moment of terror, or repeated feelings of fear, or thoughts and feelings of insecurity, tend to remain within us as a kind of sediment which inclines us to a fear mentality. But if these negative impressions have been swiftly opposed by other thoughts and positive feelings, they leave scarcely any trace within us. Note, for instance, how a frightened child is comforted by his parents or teachers. And an adult manner of dealing with a sudden fright, disgust, or failure is to reason about it and to conclude that it was not so terrible after all.

A contrary example. A little four-year-old girl, playing with a puppy, did not notice a huge dog jump over the fence, but heard it hit the ground just behind her. She was terrified, screamed, wept, ran away, and could never be near any dog without trembling with terror. I knew her years later when she was a doctor running a clinic in a capital city of the Far East. She admitted to me that the phobia was still with her and so overcame her once in a Paris restaurant that, when a man brought a dog into the restaurant, she lost control of herself and climbed up on the table out of its reach. If her mother had only done with her what another mother, better prepared for such an incident, did with her little girl! The very next day, while her little girl was eating near a door which opened onto their garden, the mother came into view at a distance leading a dog on a leash. When the little girl started to become frightened and screamed, her mother said, "Don't be afraid. This is a very good dog, and I have him on the leash." Then the little girl quieted down and went on with her dinner. Every day her mother brought the dog a little nearer, with a similar outburst of fright from the little girl, then victory over it. After about thirty such positive experiences the little girl was cured of her phobia.

Whenever the tendency stays rooted in the subconscious, it must not be allowed to grow. The opposite feelings must be implanted. The tendency will not increase if we do not continue to feed it with negative thoughts, conversations, actions, and attitudes. We shall control and eliminate it if we act out the contrary positive emotional situations. A single very strong positive feeling can sometimes be a complete cure of such a tendency.

An Example

In his youth, despite a strong and attractive personality, Francis de Sales was almost overcome by a scruple of conscience. One day, in a state bordering on despair despite repeated confessions, he went into a church and spoke to Our Lord: "If I am to hate and curse you throughout all eternity in hell, at least I want to love and praise you now in this life with all my strength." And for a good long time he gave a free rein to sentiments, previously repressed, of love of God. He walked out of that church cured of his scruple forever. This strong feeling and positive emotion of love had destroyed the negative attitude of fear and insecurity which had been causing his scrupulosity.

So, in handling these difficulties, we must especially be sure to implant the opposite feeling and tendency. Love and sympathy counteract antipathy and hatred, as we shall explain in the chapter on anger. Against insecurity and fear we should use heroic decisions, acts which embrace positive values and trains of thought which imply security. Against sadness we should repeat ideas and attitudes which are joyful. When the new, positive "sediment" produced by a positive manner of thinking and acting equals or is greater than the negative tendency which has accumulated in our interior life, then we shall be cured. If the cure is not complete, at least we shall experience definite relief.

5. Change the external expression of the feeling.
The emotion has a fulcrum in its physiological counterpart, i.e., the external expression of eyes, breathing, voice, and muscles. If you remove this support and, even better, "act out" the opposite external expression as far as possible, you weaken or extinguish the undesirable feeling.

In fear or anger the eyes become hard, staring, and blink scarcely at all. The road to victory in moments of irritation is to relax the eyes deliberately, blink often, and try to smile with the eyes. The day after I explained this to a group of college students, one of them came to me and said with enthusiasm: "Father, this is terrific. Last night I was about to lose my temper, but I remembered what you said in your talk. I relaxed my eyes and smiled with them; I took a few deep breaths and controlled myself so well that my mother, who was listening in the next room, came in afterward to congratulate me and ask me to explain to her how I did it."

In a state of emotion the voice tends to be hard and trembling. So, in a moment of wrath, you should keep quiet or answer very softly. Speak in a stronger tone of confidence when you feel fear, and in moments of sadness use a more animated tone of voice. Popular wisdom tells us all this in the proverbs of many languages. In English, the expression "To whistle in the dark" expresses a method of conquering fear. Songs are a proverbial cure for sadness even as far back as the words of St. James' Epistle. The Japanese have a more poetical expression: "When the face smiles, the sun comes out in the heart." We should, then, relax and soften the lines of facial expression and unclench tense hands in emotional moments.

All by itself this physiological control of an emotion, acting out the opposite expression of it, will often not be enough. In certain cases it may even be harmful, if we continue to hold on to the exciting thought. But if we add to physiological control the management of our spirit, by arousing contrary thoughts and feelings, victory will be swift and sure.

Putting together these two means last mentioned (contrary feelings and expressions), we come to a practical technique for overcoming deep-rooted feelings. We must live out in our imagination the circumstances that have so great an effect on us, then describe with a *tone* of conviction the emotional state in which we should be, or would like to be, or in which normal persons would be. This *tone* of security, if it is intense, will produce a proportionate *feeling* to counteract the phobia.

Father Laburu[7] tells the story about a country boy who was terrified of locusts. Whenever he saw one close by, he began to tremble, lose his wits, and run. In his case this was practically uncontrollable and he would have even thrown himself out the window if he found no other way to get out of the room. Father Laburu told him to *imagine* that a locust was flying through the door and then had him say, "I am perfectly calm," imitating a tone of security. "The locust is getting nearer," said the psychologist, and the boy repeated this after him. Imagining a locust coming closer, the boy began to be frightened. But by keeping on saying, "And I am perfectly calm; it makes no difference to me," he did grow calm. Then Father Laburu had him say, "The locust is right next to me. It is in Father's hands" (Father Laburu had brought one in a small jar). "Now it is in my hands" (he had him take in his hands the bottle with the locust); "I am perfectly calm." Scarcely had he uttered this last phrase in a tone of great control when a deep breath of relief and an open smile showed his complete liberation from the phobia. Once the first phase of emotion has been brought under control, we begin to experience the consoling effects of emo-

[7] José Antonio Laburu Olascoaga, S.J. (1887-1972), a preacher, writer, missionary, and psychologist who worked in Spain and Latin America.

tional control in body and soul both. These are the following: greater muscular relaxation, a calming down of nervousness, glandular and hormonal equilibrium. Health is preserved and improved. We feel a greater strength and serenity, and a deeper sense of joy. We gain easier victory over our lower instincts. We begin to have a stronger and more balanced personality, to know internal and social peace. Greater happiness is ours, and there is edification of our neighbor. And, finally, we please God more and work for His greater glory.

Exaggerated Impressionability

This exaggeration is a result of the fact that the *organism itself* is weakened, tense, or producing an excessive amount of certain hormones. But this exaggeration depends also, and especially, on the life of our *spirit* and the ideas and patterns of thought that have become habitual.

1. *Organic weakness:* sick people, children, women, and the elderly are usually more impressionable than a man in robust health.

2. Muscular tension opens up the way to emotion, and this tension is the first thing produced by emotion. Once this tension is present, a very small stimulus will produce emotional effects which increase rapidly. President Franklin D. Roosevelt was said to have kept a couch in his office where he stretched himself out at odd moments several times a day to relax completely for a few minutes. This muscular relaxation gave him greater equanimity and, as a result, he spoke with greater authority and assurance. Chancellor Adenauer of the Federal Republic of Germany, despite his eighty-two years, was the man responsible for his country's economic recovery.

He had a capacity for prodigious activity, equanimity, and long hours of work. He owed this to the fact that every day he took two or three short naps which relaxed all his muscles.

3. Excessive hormonal production is characteristic of one who lets himself be dominated frequently by anger, fear, or sadness. It also prepares the way for a second phase of emotion in which the glands become habitually overactive. In a word, these are the "stress illnesses" described by Dr. Selye. Whether injected or produced by the organism itself, adrenaline makes us more irritable.

Greater Impressionability

This depends especially on the life of our *spirit*, the manner in which we face life. The very same events have a great effect on some individuals, and little or no effect on others. Even in the same individual they may have great, small, or no effects, depending on antecedent circumstances or the element of surprise. Little trace is left behind in persons whose ideas, convictions, or feelings permit them to see in such events other aspects to counterbalance the sadness or fear, desire or worry. For instance, two different men, one avaricious and proud, the other disinterested and humble, suffer the same reverse of fortune and go bankrupt. The first will be very depressed and sad. If he does not know how to distract himself and face his misfortune in a positive manner, it will eventually dominate him and bring complete loss of control. The second man, however, full of positive ideas and feelings, will not experience so great a shock. When the first reaction has passed, he will almost instinctively, as it were, be able to find even happiness in his new situation.

The Root of Exaggerated Impressionability

We must seek for this on the level of our lower mental activities. These do not perceive higher realities and take us
away from the true reality of things, of life and our own
personality. Exaggerated impressionability is rooted in the
following instincts: those of self-preservation, domination,
and reproduction. There is an innate *tendency to preserve* our
physical, bodily nature by the reaction of flight from danger
and bodily death without bothering about what is spiritual
and eternal. There is also a *tendency to win out over others* and
increase our own earthly goods or reputation without taking
into account whether this impedes other still greater goods.
There is, finally, *a tendency to seek pleasure for one part* of our
being even if it be to the detriment of the whole. This is also
an impulse to flee from pain and hardship although these
may bring higher goods to us. The right to our inheritance
is sold for a mess of pottage. Sexual or alcoholic pleasure is
sought, even though ruinous to health.

Body, but Also Spirit

We do not take into account the true reality of man. Man
is not only body but spirit also. He is not only earthly and
temporal but heavenly and eternal. We do not even take
our own personality into account. For we refuse to accept
limitations imposed on us by heredity or environment. As a
result, the emotional center of gravity is thrown off balance.

This center of gravity in man is the sublime goal given
him by the Creator. Man is to dispose of himself according
to the good pleasure of the Infinite Being so that afterward
he may enjoy Him for all eternity. Whoever realizes the
sublime dignity of being able to fulfill at each moment the

ideal God sets for us, that is, "to want what He does and do what He wants," and realizes that this cannot be impeded by sickness or poverty or another's evil or injustice—such a person is less likely to suffer a lasting mental disturbance. The saints understood this sublime goal and lived it, and they are, thus, models of self-control. For this reason, too, believers who suffer emotional disturbances will do very well to add to scientific methods the still more effective methods of the *Spiritual Exercises*[8] of St. Ignatius Loyola. By meditating on this great truth in his first exercise, called the *Principle or Foundation*,[9] they will balance their center of gravity again

---

[8] A practical manual "for guidance in self-mastery and the management of life, and, to that end, for guidance in making the appropriate decisions only in moments of inner personal freedom from those emotional and other biases which militate against authentic Christianity."—paragraph #21, *The Spiritual Exercises of St. Ignatius Loyola*, trans. Lewis Delmage, S.J., New York: Joseph F. Wagner, Inc., 1968. This practical manual is frequently used in making spiritual retreats.

[9] According to St. Ignatius the *Principle or Foundation* of our whole spiritual life reads as follows:

> Man is created to this end, to praise and reverence the Lord his God and to play his own role in the Paschal Mystery. But all of sub-human reality and its relationships to man are created for man's sake, i.e., to help him achieve the end of his own creation. Hence it follows that the former are to be used or set aside to the extent that they help or hinder the achievement of the goal of life.
>
> Therefore, we should cultivate a free and independent attitude toward anything less than God or the cause of God or the promptings of the Holy Spirit regarding Christ in His members. (The only proviso is that the choice of an

and will feel their fears and worries disappear in the deepest peace of soul.

In Lima, where I received a great deal of real help in missionary propaganda from an active and businesslike lady, I stood in admiration of the serenity which the following thought habitually brought her in spite of contradictions and failures. "In comparison with God, the Infinite Being, all men are like a little grain of sand. And how much less am I? But if this atom can bring a smile to the Infinite Being, why be lost in worry about whether other atoms are praising Him or not? And why lose time thinking merely about myself, my illnesses, virtues, or defects?"

Preventive Remedy

Begin at the root cause first. Fix the hierarchy of values firmly in the understanding by a good moral and religious education. Form a correct appreciation of what is lasting and eternal as superior to what is but temporal and passing. Set the total good of your whole being above the partial good of your body

---

undertaking, situation, or instrument be up to our own discretion and within our competence, and not forbidden.)

Consequently, the result should be that, as far as we ourselves are personally concerned, we ought not to seek health for its own sake any more than illness, nor for their own sakes prefer riches to poverty, prestige to disrepute, influence to disregard, command to a subordinate position, tenure to change, nor a long life to a short one.

The fundamental principle is that in every alternative we should choose and want only what leads to the end. — paragraph #23, *The Spiritual Exercises of St. Ignatius Loyola*, *op. cit.*

alone. Illuminate and direct your instincts toward their right road and goal. Elevate them by knowledge and faith to heights with which they are themselves unacquainted.

You must strive to appreciate and work toward your total good. You must have a self-love which is not creeping, earthly, or material but higher, spiritual, and eternal. It must be a love of the life and glory which will not end, a love of suffering dignified by the ideal of bearing it as God's will, a disinterested love of others. If you have supernatural faith and charity, love your neighbor because in him you see your Creator disguised in his defects. Thus you can love and serve God with greater merit.

You can attain this by meditation on higher goods and practice of the virtues. The more you strengthen your higher mental activities by the understanding of higher values and by positive decisions for good, the more you will be immune from the disorders of lower instincts. In the case of the saints this dominion of reason and right morals reaches its culmination. Disgrace, humiliation, and temporal dangers caused them no worries whatsoever.

Secondly, in your conduct avoid any ideas or surroundings, sights or acts which favor distorted tendencies. Block unlawful satisfaction of instinct, for this engraves and stamps false values into your very being.

Integral Religious Psychotherapy

Considering the remedies indicated in this chapter, especially if we go to the depths of the problem, we might conclude that atheism, materialism, or a vague deism create a poor psychotherapy which satisfies neither heart nor reason. If we consider only man's physiology and not his spiritual soul with its aspirations toward the infinite, if we separate him from God and do not orient him toward his Maker, Father, and Eternal Happiness, then we disintegrate him psychically and separate him from reality. Then he becomes disjointed. In the most intimate part of his being there will always be a vacuum of existential anguish. The edifice of security, satisfaction, optimism, robust personality, and a realization of limitless values, which we desire to construct upon such a foundation, will have no solidity. Nor can it offer resistance to a sudden reverse of fortune.

On the other hand, a psychotherapy which is founded upon faith and the divine destiny of man calms and satisfies the reason, feelings, the soul itself, and the whole nervous system. It keeps a man normal, integral, serene, and sublime even amid the greatest suffering and in the face of death itself. Evidence for this is visible in the thousands of martyrs and saints of every age, race, and condition of life.

At the seventh International Catholic Congress of Psychotherapy held in Madrid, September 1957, a desire was evident to integrate analytic findings with the Catholic concept of man. Such an integration could perhaps be attained more easily if we followed the technique of Dr. Martinez Arango of Havana and the directive of Dr. Caruso, i.e., to consider man in his total reality as a "child of God and heir to heaven." Freud was the discoverer of a "new world" in psychotherapy. He discovered the unconscious forces in man. But since he disregarded what is spiritual and supernatural in us, he gave an excessive importance to the instinctive mechanisms of the "libido." Adler parted ways with Freud when he did not find in the teachings of his master that other great unconscious force, the instinct to "domination." He himself explained and utilized this mechanism of "domination." Jung went even further and caught a glimpse of the supernatural or the divine without, however, formulating it as anything more than an archetype or collective unconscious.[10] If these great visionaries had known that we came from God, that we are sparks from the hearth of Infinite Love, if they had understood that the insatiable thirst for love and happiness which we experience are the urgings of our Heavenly Father to transform ourselves in Him and share in His infinite happiness, perhaps then they would have conceived and explained clearly what they left indefinite, and would have avoided many inaccuracies and contradictions in their theories.

It is logical and understandable that, since man has fallen from the original elevated state in which God placed him, he should experience a certain vital anguish. But redeemed man can easily overcome such an obstacle and see that he is provided with so many means, suffering included, of elevating himself to a divine level. For whoever deals with divine wealth can scarcely be overly concerned with earthly affairs of lesser importance. In this manner we can have an easier solution to many cases of frustration, despair, phobia, disgust, conflict, repression, fixation, and worry.

---

[10] Finally, in 1932, Jung wrote, "During the last thirty years people have consulted me from all civilized regions of the world ... among all my patients in the second half of life—that is to say, over thirty-five—there has not been one whose problem in the last resort was not that of finding a religious outlook on life. It is safe to say that every one of them fell ill because he had lost that which the living religions of every age have given to their followers, and none of them has been really healed who did not regain his religious outlook."

Some Crucial Problems and Their Solution in Psychotherapy

There are some transcendental problems which consciously or unconsciously urge themselves upon every rational being and which can be, in him, the occasions of sadness, despair, and pessimism. For instance, the origin and end of the world; who made it and for whom? Who governs it? Why are we here in it? Why do we suffer and die? What happens after death?

In the synoptic table on the two following pages we shall compare the solutions and replies which are given us by atheistic or materialistic psychotherapists and the solutions and effects which religion offers us.

Psychophysiological Trajectory of Feelings

Emotions:	An emergency reaction totally disturbing our normal state of happiness.
Occasion:	Any unusual event or sensation, or the memory of it.
Cause:	The thought that affects my happiness.
Organic Effects:	Resulting from muscular tension: a disturbance in digestion, respiration, circulation, and so forth.
Psychical Effects:	Full attention: fixation, obsession, exaggeration, etc. Repeated or strong feelings. A deeply wrought tendency, e.g., neurosis.
Effects of the Hormonal Phase:	In depressive emotions: STH, asthma, arthritis, hypertension, fatigue In aggressive emotions: ACTH, malnutrition, ulcers, diabetes, infection, insomnia, etc.
Control of These Emotions:	1. Avoid the occasion or the disturbing idea. 2. Change the focal point surrounding the event, and one's own attitude and habits. 3. Discover and modify the idea. 4. Implant the opposite tendency. 5. Assume the opposite expression. 6. Correct the exaggeration in one's impressionability.
Integral Psychotherapy:	A comparison of the educational resources of psychotherapy with religion / without religion

Crucial Problems and Their Solution in Psychotherapy

Origin and Destiny of the World and Man; Suffering; Death

Solution

Atheistic and Materialistic Psychotherapy	*Religious Psychotherapy*
Does not know the origin of the world nor why it exists.	The world comes from a wise and perfect Creator to help man toward perfection.
Chance governs it, i.e., no one.	It is governed by God, a loving Father, omnipotent.
We are in it as the most perfect animals, without being able to satisfy our thirst for love, peace, joy, and accomplishment.	We are here as on a passageway toward complete happiness: • to increase it by our merits • to glorify our Infinite Father After death we shall love and enjoy God.
Suffering is inadmissible; it has no advantage. Death is annihilation, the end of everything.	Suffering perfects us and increases our reward. Death is the end of exile and entrance into our fatherland.

Effects

Does not satisfy reason: it leaves behind intellectual insecurity, doubt about what is most important and transcendental.	*Satisfies the reason:* with intellectual security and certitude about what is most important for us.

Does not satisfy the heart: it leaves behind a vacuum, anguish, sadness, emotional insecurity

- without an adequate object to love

- without a sufficient feeling of being loved and protected

- without real accomplishment to fulfill the soul's aspirations

Satisfies the heart: it gives peace, security, confidence, love, joy, and full satisfaction

- with an Infinite Goodness to love

- feeling oneself loved and protected by God

- realizing the ideal of Infinite Wisdom

Consequently:
1. Integral psychotherapy needs the spirit of God.
2. A healthy spiritual life is already a superior kind of psychotherapy; it gives us:
   a. Unity in our whole life of mind and heart
   b. Complete satisfaction and realization
   c. Security in this life and for eternity

6

Résumé of Re-educational Treatment

Once convinced that illness or weakness comes from disorders in your mental activities together with alterations in your nervous and muscular system, follow this health decalogue.

1. Begin by learning how to rest. Exercise naturally the easiest of mental acts, *conscious sensations*. This is at once a tonic and sedative. If tension and fatigue are very great, first take a few days' rest. Change your environment or occupation, or travel.

2. Then go on to perform perfectly and without tension the second, more active mental act. Concentrate your attention on *a succession* of sensations, images, or reasoning processes which you remember from the past or now elaborate in your imagination. Emphasize single-mindedness in your work.

3. In the second or third week, without wholly abandoning the previous exercises, strengthen your will by means of *decisions* that are concrete, progressively more difficult, and punctually executed. Sweep out all indecision.

4. Once your faculties are trained, correct whatever *abnormality* there may be in your feelings. To this end *first modify*

the idea or image which produces them and substitute for it (as soon as it appears in consciousness) sensations and concentrations which are clearly distinct and, so far as possible, also pleasant.

5. Then *modify* the emotional overtone of that idea or feeling which is bothering you. Do this first *by means of reasoning:* "This feeling of mine is irrational. Others are not bothered by it; it does not sadden them as much as it does me. I should react as others do, as a normal man."

6. *Associate another, different feeling* with that idea. Bring the idea consciously to mind and then imagine other consequences and live out the other feeling which you will have prepared beforehand.

7. *Arouse the contrary feeling* in yourself and make it penetrate even to the subconscious by imagining it vividly and speaking about it with the tone of voice peculiar to the feeling you wish. And work *as if* you already had it. Associate this strong feeling of security or courage, for instance, with the idea which formerly produced disturbance or fear. (Remember the case about the locust.)

8. Simultaneously with this whole treatment *repair the expenditure* of nervous and muscular energy which mental tension produces by accustoming your muscles to exercise and due relaxation. Do this both for the time of waking and sleeping. Waste no nervous energy in useless movements or tense postures.

9. *Avoid the formation of toxins* by eating foods which are readily digested, and practice regular elimination. Build up your

cells, nerves, and muscles through healthy breathing and adequate diet.

10. *Accept the reality* which cannot be modified. Found your ideal upon reality. Fill out your human ideal with sublime truths which are eternal and divine.

Applications and Practical Advice for Maladjustments of Personality

Know Yourself

Weakness or illness is no mere imagination or fiction. Symptoms felt in head, heart, or digestive apparatus are real symptoms. In general, however, they are not caused by a lesion in your organs, but by uncontrolled mental activity or the chaotic subconscious. Consult a specialist, and, if he agrees about the integrity of the organs, there should be no further worry about this decision. You must attend to and convince yourself of the fact that these symptoms owe their origin and intensity to mental causes, or to uncontrolled thought about them and about the illness which seems to afflict them.

The practical conclusion will be not to think of the symptoms or illness voluntarily. Rather practice thinking voluntarily about the clinical decision. Feel your complete health and organic efficiency. To know the mental nature of the illness and to locate the struggle on its true ground will be 50 percent of the cure. The other 50 percent is in confidence and faith in the method, together with the time factor.

Think of Others

No one who lives for himself alone lives as fully or produces as much as he who lives for others and does good for others.

When you are dominated by your unconscious mental activities, you lead a negative life which is colored by a sickly egoism. You are always thinking of your own troubles and finding ways to lessen them. You can find no time to busy yourself with others or do any positive and progressive work. You see the enemy everywhere and are wholly taken up with fleeing from him.

Such a person lives, as Fosdick puts it, as if in a room lined with mirrors. Wherever he looks he sees himself. But when he busies himself with others, several of these mirrors are changed into windows through which he can see other faces, other lives, and other more pleasant landscapes.

You will also find great help in a noble ideal. This may be professional or religious. Let it be some unselfish dedication to your work either out of patriotism, love of your neighbor, or from some religious motive.

I knew a young doctor who was exhausted by his studies and first labors. He was crushed by insomnia, obsessions, fatigue, and a sickly egoism. Then he decided to take a trip to rest and distract himself. On his arrival at a Chinese port, a missionary invited him to visit his hospital. He began to interest himself in the illnesses of those good people and lent them his professional services out of compassion. He ended up by remaining as the head of the establishment. He forgot his own ills and was completely cured.

Practice Singleness of Thought

The general cause, remote or proximate, of these mental illnesses is a kind of double thought. Or it is an occupation with several ideas at once (obsessions, fears, worries). Practice singleness of thought, then, in order not to increase your ills.

Imitate St. Bernard, the most active and busiest man of his century. On his shoulders rested the responsibility for his monastery, the composition of admirable books, consultation with princes, and even the business of the universal Church. When he entered a church he used to say, "Thoughts of Bernard, remain outside." And he would concentrate on his prayers in peace.

Practice Confidence

To lessen the force of an obsessing idea, a feeling of sadness or worry, you must oppose to it an intimate persuasion that everything in this world passes. Imagined ills are always greater in our minds than they are in reality. Fears of insanity, heart failure, or sudden death, which many nervous people have, are never realized. Experience confirms this and doctors attest to it.

Have confidence in your own health and do not be bothered by trivial symptoms of illness. Our organism is so complicated and so exposed to contrary influences that it naturally cannot function for a single day without some friction among its many parts. You may truly say, "This is nothing. It will soon pass away." Remember that however little your attention is worriedly fixed on a sensation, it is thereby disquieted, increased, and exaggerated. Conversely, when you shift attention to a different matter, the evil lessens and gradually disappears.

Never did fear or discouragement put off the arrival of threatening evils. What fear or discouragement really does when exaggerated is to dissipate and exhaust the forces and strength you need to go out and resist those evils. If they must come, let them not, by thought, begin to torture you before the time.

Profit by Moderate Discussion

Discuss the matter freely with a prudent and experienced person. Thus you will lessen the discouragement, sadness, worry, or fear, and calm the tension. Apart from discussion and consultation with specialists it is better not to speak of your illness or symptoms. The less you think of them, the less they will bother you.

This mental tyranny over you will be softened by freely talking it over with God in prayer if you accept what you have to suffer with great confidence in His love and almighty power.

Suffering is like a perfume. If you open it to human egoism, the fragrance evaporates unperceived. If you open it to God, it rises to Him like incense and comes down to you again like a heavenly dew. "To carry a splinter in one's heart," says Vicente Gar-Mar, S.J., "and talk of something else is the feat of a hero."

Exercise Conscious Life

When you are not engaged in intellectual work, rest your mind by receiving conscious sensations with an easy, peaceful attention to the things of the external world. And when doing mental work exert yourself in concentrating all your attention there. Forget the past, future, and yourself. In the beginning you will do this easily for a few moments. Then by progressive increase of attention you will attain normal concentration.

The root of the evil is in domination of conscious mental activity by the unconscious. Now the acts prescribed above are in themselves insignificant. Yet, because they are fully conscious and often repeated during the day, they attack the root of the evil directly. They produce a reaction of greater joy, peace, and mastery.

Don't Be Discouraged

Do not think it strange if in the morning you notice a greater sensation of the symptoms, discouragement, or fatigue, and if fatigue is less and sadness almost gone by the afternoon or after doing some work. The reason is that the unconscious is in control during sleep. And there is danger after awakening of continuing under its disturbing influence. After some controlled acts, however, joy returns again and our vigor is rejuvenated.

Nor should you wonder at the periodic appearance of enthusiasm and discouragement, progress and apparent setbacks. This happens in many mental and nervous illnesses.

Fight Pessimism

An uncontrolled imagination drives a man toward pessimism and exaggeration of his troubles, and hence to discouragement and despair. For sad events and experiences, at one time conscious but now perhaps forgotten, continue to be active on the unconscious level. They tend to add a pessimistic overtone to all mental images. If we reflect on our thoughts and feelings, we shall see that even insignificant beginnings can have terrifying consequences.

A brief daily examination in writing of the course of your pessimistic imaginings will quickly convince you of this. You will then belittle those fears, troubles, and worries. If you discount your fears by 90 percent, you will be closer to reality. Give no importance then to imagined ills or fears for the future. Better still, once you recognize the error or exaggeration of your unconscious mental associations, deliberately come to the opposite conclusion: enthusiasm, joy, courage, optimism. For, as Father Gar-Mar again said, the shadow of the cross is often larger than the cross itself. So black, so sad, so crushing are the crosses we dream up for ourselves.

Keep Busy

Employ your time well and so distribute it among different tasks that by keeping yourself busy you have no time for worry. To enable the factor of feeling to intervene here, let your undertakings be in the possible and practical order. Make sure they are useful and interesting. Only when the sick imagination finds the field of consciousness unoccupied will it be able to torture you with its sad and discouraging exaggerations. Idleness and the lack of an ideal produce *more neurotics* than work ever does.

A young bride, her mother told me, used to live tormented by fears. One fear was that she would lose her mind. She bore a son, and still the fears continued. In the course of time she had five more children and because she was not rich she had to do all her own housework. Hardly could a worry take shape when a child's wail would bring her flying to its side. Or two of them would start a squabble and she would be off to calm them down. Or she had to get a meal ready, or the ironing board was calling her. Or rain threatened to wet her laundry that was stretched on the line to dry. Some urgent household task would always be taking up her whole attention and coming just in time to kill worries at their first stirring.

The famous Jesuit scholar, Father Wassman, conquered his own depression by taking up the study of ants. In this field he later became so preeminent that the whole world marveled at his books.

Foster Joy and Optimism

Insist upon joy and optimism as opposed to the sadness and discouragement which sometimes seem so natural. Do this by briefly changing your occupation and busying yourself with thoughts, readings, and conversations which make the mind happy and elevate it. Do not pretend to drown melancholy in alcohol for, as a modern author says, drinking does not drown our troubles but only irrigates them.

The central powerhouse which supplies current to our organs is optimism, either instinctive or acquired. Feelings of joy and health stimulate blood circulation and accelerate nutritional processes. If you doubt your forces and think yourself sick, you are already beginning to be sick. Then the central powerhouse has lowered its potential. All lights grow dim. Your organs do not work so well. Sad passions, such as fear, worry, discouragement, agitation, anger, scorn, anxiety, make us realize the truth in the common phrase "It makes me sick!"

All joy is curative and all discouragement tends to increase our troubles. Gladness is a swimming pool of health where we should bathe each day. Chapter 14 of this book (on happiness) will help you produce this effect.

Get Down to Work

If you suffer from any of these personality maladjustments remember that there is no lesion in your higher faculties, above all in your will. What happens is that you do not know how to use them. These faculties are marvelous forces. When well directed they are capable of transforming any mental pattern and curing any abnormality. But you must know how to avail yourself of their benefits. This is easily attained by re-education. You have the cure in your own hands. A little constancy and method is enough.

Your thoughts are the limit of your activities. No one takes a single step further than his convictions. If you imagine to yourself that you cannot do this or that, you will never do it. *"Possunt quia posse videntur,"* the old Romans used to say. "They can because they think they can." Aside from the times when you need the ministrations or advice of a professional physician, your six best doctors are sun, water, air, exercise, diet, and joy. They are always there waiting for you. They cure your ills and do not cost you a cent.

Part 2

Re-education and Applications

The kind of life many of us are forced to live in the modern world is fatiguing and hinders rest even in sleep. It makes tranquil and deep thought more difficult. It stifles the will and confuses acts of the will with mere impulses. It exalts feelings, lets the sexual instinct run riot, kills all deep satisfaction and true happiness. It deadens or annihilates ideals. The following applications and methods of re-education, personality readjustment, and self-completion follow logically from the first part of this book.

7

How to Rest

Whoever knows how to rest at the right time will
double his efficiency and not waste his health.

Rest means the suspension of work and energy output, the recuperation of energy and building up of reserve forces. We must learn how to rest: (A) *While awake:* at odd moments, during meal times, while traveling, during the time of recreation, as part of our social and religious life, and even at certain moments during our work itself. We must also learn how to rest: (B) *During the hours of sleep.*

While Awake
1. In an acute crisis of "overwork" or nervous fatigue.
2. In normal fatigue.

1. Nervous Fatigue
We can consider the brain cells as accumulators of energy. They are normally charged when the blood carries oxygen and nutrition to them during the repose of sleep. This would also take place on other occasions when we maintain a mental and emotional disinterestedness while also in a state of

muscular relaxation. This is a comparison or theory not yet scientifically proven, but put forward as a hypothesis. These cells would discharge their energy whenever we turn our active attention upon anything.

This discharge of energy is slow and almost imperceptible in the spontaneous and peaceful attention had in conscious sensations or simple concentration. It is something like electricity consumed by a lamp of low wattage. Then the brain cells hardly consume any appreciable amount of our energy.

The discharge of energy will be greater and more noticeable in the case of violent or forced attention (compare burning a high-powered electric light). Another instance would be the case of having one thing at the center of our conscious attention (e.g., something that we hear or read) and, at the same time, some other subconscious center of attention such as a vague scruple, a hidden problem, a stifled fear or disgust, or a need to hurry (compare two candles, one well lit and the other sputtering). The brain cells are expending more energy than normal.

But the discharge of energy will be most rapid when, instead of a single lamp or a lamp and a half, two lights are burning full power at the same time. That is to say, when we have two centers of conscious attention, as a person who wants to pay attention to several matters at the same time![11] Now the brain cells are consuming even their reserve energy.

[11] Probably there is no such thing as a simultaneous and fully conscious attention to two or more matters at the same time, but rather a *very rapid shift back and forth* from one idea to another.

If the battery power is greatly expended but not entirely, because we interrupt it in time or because we soon correct the double attention, we do feel mental fatigue, but we recuperate easily. The fatigue will be greater and recuperation more difficult if our reserves become exhausted. This will especially be true if the "accumulator" is only half charged because of an illness or general weakness, or because the forced attention is prolonged a great deal, or because the "double lamp" consumes too much energy.

A student may already be exhausted by successive nights of forced study just before an examination. Or a businessman or professional man may be nervous and irritated to the point of exploding because of worry, anxiety, and hurrying. If either of these goes on demanding more and more energy from himself, his cells will have had no time to replenish themselves and will have nothing more to give. They will go on to consume their very substance in order to provide all the energy possible, and he will soon experience true exhaustion or "surmenage" (overwork). This is more difficult to cure as the internal self-consumption has progressed. In extreme cases some tissues can even start to break down. Then the feeling of fatigue, accompanied by a sensation of heaviness or heat in the forehead or around the eyes, and followed by sad and depressing ideas, is unusually intense and difficult to control. Consequently, the first remedy is to take adequate means to get the patient to forget himself and his illness. Specialists obtain this effect organically and violently by injections or electric shocks which produce forgetfulness or artificial sleep. However, in many less serious cases we need not take such extreme measures. Similar results can be obtained through less violent and more natural means; for example, a few days' travel or a change of dwelling or occupation. Enliven yourself with amusements which will arouse enthusiasm and prevent depressing memories. Avoid remaining inactive or unoccupied. Idleness is no solution. If depressing feelings find the field of consciousness unoccupied they will at once occupy it themselves and begin to torment you. In short, be objective. Act during the day as a receiver of impressions from the external world so that you give no place or time to the interior world of subjective thoughts and feelings. Later on let the work of re-education begin by means of conscious sensations and voluntary concentrations.

In Normal Fatigue

Since this comes from the working of your productive power, make yourself receptive by means of conscious sensations.

Apply the sense of *sight.* Let the object penetrate within you exactly as it is, without subjective modifications. Make no comparisons. Do not reason about causes and effects. Otherwise you will still be producing ideas. Look at things just as children do, naturally, without anxiety, without wanting to embrace all the details. Contemplate, for example, a lamp, a landscape, a flower, a color, the details of some object. Get the overall effect. Absorb yourself in it. With practice this will, day by day, become easier and more successful.

Hear a near or distant noise. Retain consciousness of it for a few seconds. Or even notice the lack of noise. Open up the sense of hearing without forced attention. Repeat these acts five times each hour of the day. With these exercises you can calm irritation and hypersensitivity to sound.

Touch and feel the coldness or hardness of five objects. In each case notice the first impression on the sense.

Walk slowly, deliberately. An excellent relaxing exercise is that used by a student who had a bad case of overwork. He could scarcely pay attention to what he was doing for more than three quarters of an hour. He had to attend three classes a day which were interrupted by five-minute recess periods. These he dedicated to scientific breathing and exercise. He would take five steps while inhaling deeply through the nose, feeling the air in the upper part of the nose near the forehead (not at the nostril openings for this closes them). Then he would exhale smoothly and passively through the mouth while taking eight or ten steps more. Meanwhile he kept his attention on hearing the air as it passed through his nose, and on feeling his steps. By thus keeping himself *merely receptive* for the space of five minutes he would rest from the preceding class. The pure air and increased circulation of his blood freed his system of many toxins.

Rest by the right use of leisure time.[12] As we have said before, idleness is no solution. (Doubtless you have also heard it called "the devil's workshop.") In both normal and excessive fatigue "just doing nothing" brings no real rest. A change of occupation is more restful than merely stopping work. The right use of leisure time will do much for your health, happiness, efficiency, concentration, and longevity. You will become more interested and more interesting.

---

[12] The translator has thought the "change of occupation" idea, several times indicated by the author, so worth emphasizing in a place of its own that he has taken the liberty of inserting this and the following paragraph. To the reader is recommended the brilliant essay of Josef Pieper, *Leisure, the Basis of Culture* (New York: Pantheon, 1952).

Manual workers should make a hobby of one of the fine arts, one of the sciences, social work, a parish activity, or investigate the world of books or new fields of knowledge. Those, on the other hand, whose work is mostly intellectual should, for part of their leisure time, take up some outdoor occupation or hobby which involves more or less vigorous physical exercise. If this is difficult they should at least make a hobby of some manual skill (one of the handicrafts or applied arts). Those who must work with their heads will thus gain greater benefit than by merely turning to some different field of intellectual endeavor. They should also do something with their hands.

You can rest from excessive work by engulfing yourself in studies or occupations or hobbies which amuse and interest you. In these you will easily obtain tranquil and perfect concentration. Another way is deliberately to experience some affection; for example, love of parents, brothers, or sisters. This is why a mother who loves her child really rests while working for him. Acts of reverence, confidence, love of God in prayer also produce these good effects. Try to have a loving feeling of His Divine Presence everywhere, especially in yourself and your neighbors, through sanctifying grace.

Bodily Relaxation

The foregoing exercises will help to avoid mental tension. But joined with this tension or caused by it, there is another, a muscular and nervous tension in hands, feet, and diaphragm, and especially in the eyes. If through proper exercises you relax these members suitably, you will experience greater mental rest.

Nervous and muscular rest. Tension, worry, and overexertion easily have repercussions throughout the whole nervous system, and more especially in the eyes, by putting into a state of abnormal contraction the nerves and muscles which are scarcely ever wholly relaxed even in sleep. If you relax your mind, you will more easily relax those muscles. Likewise, if you let muscles and nerves go loose and limp, your mind will be relaxed and relieved. Since the soul is intimately united to the body, it is logical that any modification in one will modify and influence the other.

You should then relax every muscle. Let them go limp. Begin with the forehead. This will lose its wrinkles or nervous contractions if you loosen up the eyes, letting the eyelids softly fall over them. Continue with the mouth, letting the corners curve up, not down. Loosen up the tongue (make a sagging face). Let the hands fall softly and leave the fingers loose and limp. Place your foot on the ground with no extra effort. Loosen the muscles of neck, jaws, chest, and abdomen. This is also an ideal exercise for inducing sleep. Gymnastic exercises and massaging can also produce this relaxation.

Rest by rhythmical breathing. This includes three steps: inhaling, exhaling, then resting motionless. The greatest relaxation is had at the third moment.

One day in New York, after having given four lectures, I found myself exhausted by mid-afternoon with two other lectures still to give. I stretched out on a couch, breathed in deliberately, exhaled naturally, and then deliberately rested for some moments until the body demanded another intake of air. During these brief moments of rest, I deliberately relaxed my eyes, forehead, and all my muscles. After a few breaths, I fell asleep. Ten minutes later I woke up completely refreshed and with the same mental lucidity as if I had spent a night in bed.

Resting the vision. The eyeball's many nerves and accommodation muscles grow tense through worry, anxiety, or mental tension. If you do not relax them before going to bed, they will not loosen up at all during sleep, especially if the previous tension has been profound or prolonged. When this goes on for weeks and months, they finally lose their elasticity. They will then be unable to accommodate the eye as they should. Farsightedness, nearsightedness, and bad focusing will result. In order to relax them we here propose several exercises recommended by experience and by the eye specialist Dr. Bates.

1. *Palming.* Sit down comfortably and relax your whole body. Let your eyelids fall softly and close the eyes without pressure. Think of the eyeball as soft, limp, and free of tension. Think that a smile is spreading evenly throughout the closed eyes. Imagine there is no light at all in them, that everything is soft and black. Cover them with the palms of your hands. Cup your hands a little so as not to press on the eyeball. Put your knees rather close together and lean your elbows on them. Relax the breathing muscles.

   The important thing is for the eyes to be closed, well covered, and as relaxed as possible. The blacker the color seen, the better relaxation and rest. Your mind should also rest at the same time. Either let it wander on pleasant subjects or imagine that the darkness is growing blacker and blacker. Ten or

twenty minutes of this two or three times a day
will produce great bodily and mental rest and will
sometimes alleviate and even cure farsightedness.

If you are agitated or tired at bedtime, you
should sacrifice a part of your sleep in order to relax
your eyes. As a result you will sleep much better.

2. *Blinking.* Do this for about ten seconds. This rest
   nature claims spontaneously. Fixed, staring eyes
   are positively unnatural. This is a harmful habit
   and causes fatigue and tension.

3. *Cold-water baths.* This relaxing effect can also be
   obtained by splashing a few handfuls of water on
   your closed eyes.

After these exercises open your eyes and take a look
around. Let the vision of an object or book come to you of
itself and rest within your eye. Do not, as it were, reach out
after it. Effort to see hinders our seeing well.

The normal eye does not attempt to see a large amount
all at the same time. Practice looking, for example, not at a
whole line but at a word or phrase. The eyes' movements are
so rapid that we get the impression that they cover a great
space at once. But when you try to see everything at once,
your eyes are in a state of tension. Relax and let them go limp
if you wish to see without fatigue. In reading you should use
your eyes as you do in writing. You do not then put on the
pressure but watch each word as you write it. So, in reading
and seeing, you should take in every detail in its own time
and not be in a hurry to see the whole thing at once.

After all illnesses the eyes, too, are convalescent. In a general weakness or fatigue these, too, are weak. At such times
you should not make them work as if they were in perfect

condition. Reading is one of the most difficult tasks for the eyes. The sick should read only a little bit or for short spaces of time. They should frequently close their eyes for a few minutes' rest. They should never make an effort to read. If you are suffering from mental or nervous fatigue, you should never read without first resting for fifteen minutes of sleep or for twenty minutes with your eyes closed. Then read with your eyes relaxed. Read for only a short time at a stretch and stop for rest when you come to periods or paragraph endings.

Rest While Asleep

Sleep, as we said above, includes both a suspension of work, which is the discharge of energy, and the recuperation of energy and reserve strength. This is most perfectly accomplished by perfect sleep without dreams or nightmares. The reasons for this follow:

1. In sleep the work of the brain is suspended (thoughts, images, feelings) and especially its function of relating to one another the different experiences of life. Only automatic movements take place and changes of bodily position. If any muscle is not sufficiently relaxed, we feel pain or stiffness in it when we waken. During sleep spontaneous sensations and subconscious life diminish and even cease in proportion to the depth of the sleep and the extent of our muscular relaxation.

2. In sleep the functions of our vegetative life diminish without being suspended. Respiration is slower, deeper, and more rhythmical. Less blood circulates to the brain. Throughout the whole organism the discharge of energy is minimal.

3. On the other hand, there is an increase in the
   recuperating activity of the nerve cells and blood
   (more red blood cells are produced). The body's
   defenses against microbes are more efficient and
   impurities are eliminated from the bloodstream
   by the activity of liver and kidneys.

Distinction between rest and sleep. Without rest we cannot live;
without sleep we can. In other words, without suspending
the discharge of energy and without recuperating energy, we
cannot for long maintain our activity or even our life. But
even without a complete loss of consciousness, if we do stay
in bed with absolute disinterestedness and mental peace and
perfect muscular relaxation, we can achieve 80 percent, 90
percent, or greater recuperation during the night. If we call
perfect sleep "100 percent rest," we would credit a restless
sleep or one with nightmares with no more than 70 percent
or 60 percent recuperation.

Consequently, we need not worry so much about insomnia. Rather we should learn how to rest well. In other words,
we should not go to bed to sleep, but to rest. We should pay
more attention to the quality of sleep than to its quantity.
Five hours of perfect rest would often be enough to make
up for daily fatigue. Even if we do not sleep at all, but stay
in bed and deliberately relax all our muscles (which often
maintain a residual tension even in sleep), we shall learn how
to obtain a greater degree of rest in the future. In such a state
of perfect relaxation we can achieve a high degree of mental
and emotional stasis and recuperate almost as much energy
as if we had spent the night in sleep. And on the following
day we shall be able to work normally.

The head of a large college began to suffer from insomnia because of illness. At first he was a bit worried. But then he said to himself, "If I can't sleep, at least I am going to rest in bed." He went about this with perfect bodily relaxation and peace of mind. Weeks and months passed without this forcing him to give up his job. He admitted to me that for six months he could not remember having slept for a minute with total lack of consciousness. When he finally lost his fears of insomnia and no longer worried about the absence of sleep, gradually sleep began to return to him.

Sleep with nightmares is no longer perfect repose. For the brain is then unconsciously working in a state of anxiety. This situation can even cause fatigue. Calm dreams, however, as demonstrated by the electroencephalograph, are quite normal.

Duration of sleep. This should vary according to the age and constitution of each individual. As a general norm we can say that when the organism is in a period of development more than seven hours seems needful. Babies and little children need more than ten. Adolescents should have from eight to ten, and young people from seven to eight. For adults seven hours are recommended, although, according to noted authors and the experience of many, only five hours would be sufficient. Total satiation with sleep makes some nervous people more apt to lose control because they find it more difficult to go to sleep next time.

Nightmares and Insomnia

The cause of dreams can be bodily (a position of the body which oppresses the heart, bad digestion, general weakness) or mental. The latter may be lack of control over the day's acts and ideas, especially those which immediately precede sleep, or working with concomitant anxiety or parasite ideas, or strong impressions, worries, emotional conflicts, unresolved problems, remorse of conscience, or strong impressions from movies, novels, or horror stories.

External circumstances are an occasion, rather than the cause, of insomnia. We know this because in identical circumstances some people will sleep while others do not. Examples of such external circumstances are mosquitoes, loud noises, someone else's snoring, too much light, heat, or cold, a strange bed, and so forth. Certain internal circumstances may also prevent sleep, such as sickness, hardening of the arteries, advanced rheumatism, toothache, stomachache, bad circulation, or too much alcohol, tobacco, or coffee.

Causes of Insomnia

Physiological cause. Observe someone asleep in a chair, his eyes closed, his head drooping, his arms and fingers relaxed. This observation tells us that we must relax the muscles in order to sleep. If these remain tense, sleep will be difficult. Muscular tension, then, is the immediate physiological cause of insomnia. But muscular tension is a result of nervous excitement deriving from ideas and feelings.

The physiological mechanism responsible for sleep has not been isolated. Many have believed that sleep is due to a separation of the dendrites (nerve endings) or an interruption of nerve currents which takes place when conscious activity ceases. Others explain it in terms of a harmony between the activity of the sympathetic and parasympathetic nervous systems.[13] When the activity of the first which predominates in the state of wakefulness is checked or diminished by mental tranquillity and relaxation, it comes into equilibrium with the activity of the second until sleep is finally produced. The part played by the hypothalamus in this procedure is generally admitted today.

Mental cause. In any theory, however, what produces this excitation or overactivity of the sympathetic nervous system is excessive work on the part of your productive power. Today it may be an uncontrolled fixed idea or an associated train of ideas corresponding to what you see and hear during the day. Tomorrow it may be some emotional conflict or a simple fear of the insomnia experienced before. Another time it might be an annoyingly unpleasant noise, such as another person's snoring or a neighbor's radio.

It is a big mistake to say, "Go to sleep quickly for there isn't much time." Given to a person (or to oneself) on the way to bed, this order is more likely to produce the opposite effect. Because going to sleep is an unconscious process, we make it more difficult by trying to bring the will into it. The less you think about it, the better. Sleep is like your shadow; if you go after it, it flees from you.

---

[13] The *sympathetic* nervous system is made up of two cords, one on either side of the spinal column, and connected by nerve fibers with the external blood vessels, glands, smooth muscles, etc. One of its functions is to speed up the heart.

The *parasympathetic* nervous system is made up of two groups of nerves arising in the cranial and sacral regions respectively. These have among their functions the constricting of the pupils, dilating of blood vessels, slowing of the heart, and increasing the action of the glands and digestive and reproductive organs.

Remedies for Insomnia

Drugs and sleeping pills. These are not cures, but palliatives. They merely help us to get out of a difficulty. They should be used only in exceptional cases, for a brief time, and under medical direction. They do not cure, but leave us weaker in the struggle against insomnia. The true remedy is a double one: the elimination of mental and nervous excitement, and muscular relaxation.

Mental Rest

1. *Eliminate mental connections.* When going to bed you should put up the following imaginary sign to oppose your worries, excitements, or business of the day: "Closed temporarily for repairs." In other words, you have to cut every mental or emotional connection with the day's events. Let every idea slip away. Let no thought bring you fear or desire. When you have pressing problems, serious worries, or emotional conflicts, you must find their solution beforehand. Bedtime is not the time to look for the answers. At most you should then decide to wait till the next day to solve or accept them.

2. *Eliminate a fixed idea or train of ideas.* Once in bed, or just beforehand, repel this fixed idea or interrupt the train of ideas by filling your consciousness with sensations (receptive mental activity). If there is an emotional conflict, discover where it is and dissolve it in the same way.

3. *Eliminate the subconscious fear of not sleeping.* After a night or several nights of insomnia you go to bed with a fear and anxiety about not sleeping. This may also be present even when you seem to have an interior resignation. Your breathing is not entirely free or deep. Your muscular relaxation is not

complete. This anxiety or fear is what is enslaving you. Even though it seems strange, the best remedy is to ask you *to will not to sleep* for a fixed length of time (one or two hours). If your decision or promise is sincere, you will notice at once that the hidden anxiety is gone. The breathing which was rather short before is now more natural and deeper. Once the fear of not sleeping is gone (now that you yourself *want* not to sleep), your productive power stops working on that idea. The activity of your sympathetic nervous system diminishes, and you consequently feel the sensation of sleep coming on. But, notice, you should be faithful to your pledge and resist sleep during the time determined. Otherwise the penalty will be to make this remedy useless when another occasion arises. If the fear reappears when you try to go to sleep again, repeat the same procedure even if you have to sacrifice several hours, or a whole night or several nights. It is certain that you will win out in the end.

Do not give too much importance to sleep by thinking that a certain number of hours is indispensable. Sometimes a simple mental sleep is sufficient (making yourself merely receptive, with muscular relaxation and rhythmic breathing). Edison, the inventor, used to work all night, but would take several ten-minute catnaps during the day.

Bodily Rest

Relax the muscles: The organic part of the remedy is to relax all the muscles, beginning with the eyes.

1. *The eyes should only be closed, without any pressure.* This is easy when we go to bed in normal fatigue, but becomes difficult when sleep does not come as soon as usual. Similarly when

we awaken in the middle of the night or at early dawn and wish to go back to sleep. Then the danger is that we shall try to force the eyes shut. Instead, keep them open but relaxed until they close of themselves.

2. *The eyes themselves should be relaxed and not fixed or staring behind the eyelids.* Pretend that you are looking up and back or that you are letting them turn up and back. This will help you to relax the muscles which control the eyeballs.

3. *To help the other facial muscles to relax, make a kind of sagging face.* Let the lower jaw droop, the cheeks and upper lip rise a bit, and the tongue lie upon the lower jaw (and not compressed against the upper part of the mouth). Some people sleep with their jaws clenched. When they go to bed, they should yawn deliberately a few times, opening the mouth wide. Yawning is a good sleep producer because of the perfect breathing and relaxation it induces.

4. *Relax the other muscles, too:* parts of the neck, arms, hands, legs, feet, and toes. Let them lie as if they were dead, without any movement, with only the pull of gravity affecting them.

5. *Imitate the slow, deep and rhythmical breathing of a sleeper,* keeping these three steps: inhaling, exhaling, then resting before you inhale again until the organism needs another breath. At such moments of rest you will notice that you can relax your eyes, forehead, etc., much more easily. Many people who tried this method after hearing one of my lectures told me later that they fell asleep after the tenth breath, even after suffering from insomnia for years.

6. *Calm yourself.* If there has been great nervous excitement before going to bed, for instance after a public appearance, a great

fright, a quarrel, or after losing one's temper, you must calm down and get the excitement under control *before* going to bed. Twenty minutes are enough for this if you prevent your memory from getting you excited all over again. For about twenty minutes practice conscious acts or conscious sensations or concentrate your attention on something easy and pleasant. Then you will be able to calm down after the greatest excitement.

7. *Eliminate the annoyance of noise.* When you find you are annoyed by a noise (another's snoring, traffic noises, the ticking of a clock, a neighbor's radio), notice that the racket is not the cause but only a condition of insomnia. For we sleep on a train with a great deal more noise going on. The immediate and true cause is the ideas which the noise awakens in us and which we do not control (indignation, impatience, anxiety to sleep). The remedy lies in willing to hear the noise. Make yourself a voluntary receiver of it, without subjectively modifying it with other ideas. The sense of hearing has sound as its proper object. It should then be able to find its satisfaction in it.

During a pilgrimage I was sharing my room with another. Hardly had he gone to bed than he began to snore loudly enough to wake the dead. At first I started to be impatient. Then I applied the remedy. I willed to listen to the snoring and hear it clearly, tranquilly observed it, and a little later fell asleep. Waking up once during the night (the noise was terrific), I used the same method again and returned to sleep.

Other Bodily Aids

1. Early rising and physical exercises during the day.
2. A frugal evening meal: milk, eggs, vegetables rich in vitamins, phosphorus, and calcium; few fats or fried foods.

3. Digestion finished before bedtime.
4. After supper avoid prolonged or taxing mental work.
5. A moderate walk in the evening or simple gymnastics just before going to bed.
6. If there is tension in the eyes, practice "palming" them.
7. Provoke yawning by opening the mouth wide and stretching the throat.
8. Sometimes it is helpful to bathe one's face or take a shower followed by a brisk toweling. This calms the nerves and brings more blood to the skin.
9. No serious reading in bed.

Résumé on Sleep

Before going to bed: avoid excitement or strong emotions. If they happen, calm down before you go to bed.

Going to bed: (1) mental and emotional stasis; (2) relax the muscles beginning with eyes, forehead, jaw, etc.; (3) breathe rhythmically, slowly and deeply, imitating a sleeper; (4) pay attention calmly to your breathing and relaxation.

In bed: (1) know how to use mental rest as well as sleep; (2) do not make sleep itself too important.

Avoid Voice Fatigue

Many orators, teachers, actors, singers, and other professional public speakers (and this can happen even as a result of prolonged private conversation) talk for a long time in a loud voice and then feel fatigue, a sensation of oppression in the chest, throat irritation or hoarseness, and sometimes back pain and other discomforts. They force their voice unnaturally and become exhausted after a half hour of speaking in public. Many have abandoned their profession or crippled their performance for this very reason. If they only knew the organic and mental causes of this defect, they could correct it.

The immediate cause is organic, i.e., defective breathing due to muscular tension. And the root of this tension is connected with uncontrolled emotions. A good voice is based upon a column of air which is kept steady by the abdominal and back muscles and goes out of the nose and mouth without impediment. The voice will not be robust and natural unless the column of air has enough pressure, can be kept steady for the length of a paragraph, and there is no physical impediment to its projection.

Organic cause. The organic cause is defective breathing because of muscular tension; above all we need an abundant supply of air.

1. There will not be *an abundant supply of air* if there is tension in nose and throat. If the nostrils are pinched together because of an emotional condition, obviously the intake of air will not be strong enough. In such instances we try to compensate by forcing the throat and vocal cords, and this produces fatigue. First of all, then, we must try to open up the nasal passages, especially up above near the eyes. A nose "like a rabbit's" should be the motto, both for inhaling and exhaling.
2. *A solid base for the column of air.* The base is not there unless the muscles of the lower abdomen and back are well expanded. To expand them,

practice breathing from the diaphragm. To check that this is being done correctly place your hands flat against your sides and the fingers will tend to separate when you inhale. Also try to widen the lower curvature of the back. These muscles also come into play by a reflex action whenever we hold the cheek muscles high and keep the nasal passages and palate well open.

3. *A steady column of air.* The whole air supply should not be gone when we pronounce a single word or phrase. And so we should keep the ribs and lower abdomen dilated and relax them a little bit at a time. Above all we must keep the nasal passages open.

4. *The air should be projected without any nasal impediments.* It should vibrate a little while we are speaking. The words should come out as if they were blown out or as if we were throwing them out in front of our eyes. The muscles around the cheekbones must not be squeezed down, nor the upper lip be tense, and the mouth should be opened wide.

5. *We should relax other tensions in the chest, shoulders, and shoulder blades; otherwise we lessen the chest capacity.* Hold the shoulders back and low. The shoulder blades should tend to come together. The rear part of the chest should be lightly elevated rather than thrown out in front, and the lower abdomen somewhat tense. Check that your posture is correct by standing up against a wall with heels back against the wall, and shoulders and head against the wall, naturally and without excessive tension.

In many persons who lead a sedentary life, the muscles of waist and back become tense and cramp their breathing. They should practice exercises or massage which relax the waist and back.

Mental or emotional cause. Emotional states such as terror, worry, hurry, discouragement, anger, and so forth tend to shorten our breath. They prevent it from beginning in the lower abdomen as it should. They tighten up the lower curvature of the back and make that difficult to expand. The shoulders rise and bend forward. The lungs, the lower lip, and the corners of the mouth all droop. As a result air does not enter or leave with ease. Hence, the voice's resonance and volume are lost; for these depend upon all the breathing muscles being flexible. You may recall the awkward tone of voice of timid people. The positive emotions, on the other hand, of love, joy, security, and optimism dilate the chest and lungs, make us breathe better, and help us to produce vocal tones more freely and purely.

Practical Exercises for Relaxing the Voice

First adopt the correct posture as indicated above: body erect, lower abdomen not protruding, lower back straight, upper chest expanded, shoulders held back and low, shoulder blades close together, facial muscles relaxed, upper lip and cheek muscles raised, nose and throat opened.

1. Breathe deliberately through the nose and let the air come out naturally through the nose (ten times or so).
2. Breathe the same way, but, as the air comes out through the nose, hum lightly until you feel the

nasal passages vibrate (ten times or so). Repeat this exercise several times a day for several days until it becomes a habit.

3. Do the same thing, but add after the hum an "O" and then an "A," letting the "O" and the "A" resonate in the head and forehead.
4. Hum again, adding E, I, U.
5. Hum: "ta, te, ti, to, tu." Hum: "ba, be, bi, bo, bu," etc.
6. First produce the humming vibration, then read aloud a few words or phrases or an entire paragraph, preserving the same "hum" attitude in the face.

Especially when speaking in public you should open your mouth wide, put a great deal of movement in your lips, breathe through mouth and nose both, and pronounce all syllables decisively and distinctly. This will be more easily done, through spontaneous reflexes, when you have trained your whole body to hold a correct posture habitually.

OUTLINE DIAGRAM

How to Rest

Rest	1. Stopping the discharge of energy	Normal discharge with one idea Abnormal discharge with two ideas	
	2. Recuperating energy by	Tranquil sleep Disturbed sleep Relaxation (disinterestedness)	100% rest 60–70% rest 90% rest

While awake	Abnormal fatigue or exhaustion	Forgetfulness: drugs, change of occupation	
		Re-education	Not by idleness or a stress on subjective life
			But by pleasant conscious activity
	In normal fatigue	Conscious sensations and conscious activity Pleasant concentrations Exercise and breathing Relaxing the muscles and eyes Moderate affection	
	What to look for	Not sleep but rest Not quantity but quality	

In sleep	Duration	Depending on the climate, one's temperament, or job:
		• a mature organism: 5–7 hours
		• a developing organism (children, adolescents): 8–12 hours
	Causes of dreams	Sleeping positions, weakness, illness Problems, emotions, excitement
	Sleeping position	Head to one side, mouth shut, no nervous tossing Good support from mattress, full relaxation
	Occasion: bodily causes	Noises, etc. Tension, excitement, activity of the hypothalamus
Insomnia	Mental causes	Emotions, problems, strong feelings, boiling ideas, anxiety to sleep, fear of insomnia
	Remedies	Mental and emotional disinterestedness Relaxation of eyes, face, limbs
Voice fatigue		Surface cause: defective breathing and muscular tension Deeper cause: emotional crises Remedies and practical exercises

8

Use of the Will

Irrational animals come perfect from the hand of the Creator. By merely following their instincts they develop and reach their goal. They have no need of education. But man is born incomplete. If he follows his animal instinct alone, he weakens himself, sickens and dies. For this purpose God gives him reason, first that of his parents and teachers, then afterward his own. God says to him, "Complete yourself." Man's duty then will always be to perfect, educate, complete, and gain the mastery of himself.

The need for education is founded in the struggle between the lower level of mental activity and the higher. The lower level has an appetite only for sense goods, even to the prejudice of higher goods. The higher level of mental activity is capable of knowing and attaining higher goods which are beyond normal sensible experience, are true and eternal. These are goods of the soul, social goods and divine goods.

The Will and Mental Activity

As a compass (or sort of gunsight) for direction in your own education or that of another, keep in mind these two principles: (1) intense mental acts remain behind within us, and (2) there is a triple scale of values in normal mental activity.

The Persistence of Mental Acts

Every intense mental act contributes to formation or deformation of personality or character. It remains associated with acts which preceded it. Even though unconscious or forgotten, it continues to influence your personality by making related acts more easy and contrary ones more difficult. For the same reason virtues practiced in childhood or at any other time will form within your personality a definite framework of mind. By this you are more apt to act well and efficiently than if this practice had never existed. Likewise a transgression or concession to exaggerated instincts, even if made only once and during youthful folly and even with a resolve to return straightway to the right road, will leave forever within your mental framework a greater inclination to evil and less ease in doing good. A single fault or passing sin is then of no little importance. This is true even though it later incurs no penalty. Nor is any act of virtue unimportant even if it is hidden or unrewarded.

Triple Scale of Values in Normal Mental Activity

The whole should prevail over the part. Just as we amputate a gangrenous limb in order to save the whole body, so partial tendencies must be subordinated to the activity of the whole. The special difficulty here arises from the following.

1. You are dependent on matter as regards food, rest, and bodily appetites. These must be brought into harmony with the spirituality of the soul. Hence,

we must restrain gluttony (our tendency to eat or drink too much) in order to care for the health of body and vigor of soul by means of temperance and even fasting. Hence, too, we must overcome sloth, our exaggerated tendency to get too much rest, or toward pleasant pastimes or entertainment. This we do by diligent and disciplined activity. Hence, in addition, we must control the sexual instinct by submitting it through chastity to reason and God's law. We must sacrifice the pleasure of a moment and only one part of the body for the total good of the same. At stake here are mental lucidity, an elevated effective life, and especially the temporal and eternal good of one's soul (see the following chapters).

2. Our subjection to automatism (tics, fears, spontaneous exaggerated disgusts), slavery to vice or to long-standing habits, exaggerated respect for what others do or "what they will say," all tend to take the place of our higher liberty and what reason or God has shown us to be obligatory or truly satisfying. ("Judge for yourselves," said the Apostles to the chiefs of the synagogue, "whether it be reasonable for us to obey you or God.") Every form of dictatorship or totalitarianism, and especially Communism, tends to annihilate such true liberty.

3. The course of our thinking is fantastic when under the influence of emotion. But this must be harmonized with objective truth. Hence, we must regain control of an uncontrolled imagination or a

tendency to daydream, of exaggerated fears or sadness, or the hatreds and antipathies which deform reality for us. Even schisms and heresies have had their origin more in emotion than in objective reasoning.

What is objective and real should prevail over what is subjective. In the beginning a child lives enclosed in his own personality. He does not want to do service or give himself. He is an egoist, merely subjective. Normal development or education will bring him to the recognition and realization of objective and social values. He will then make them his norm of action. From his social isolation he will lean toward whoever offers him support. He will want to change himself into a useful and working member of the community. Only a morbid mental pattern will make a man an egoist.

Development should be continuous. Your whole being tends to develop progressively, become the master of itself, realize its ideal gradually. The memory, understanding, and even the muscles tend to atrophy if they are not used. A professional man who neglects to perfect his knowledge becomes ineffective and incompetent. On the road of virtue, too, not to go forward is to turn back. Whole civilizations have become drunk with the thought of progress achieved; then at once they began to crumble. Stagnation, softness, and vice conquered the Roman Empire more than the barbarians from the north.

You may draw important ascetical conclusions from these principles. (1) If you give up self-conquest and mortification as a means of rising from vice or sin, there will be a regression in your development or progress. (2) The "liberation of your personality toward objective values" (that is, society or God) is in psychology what in asceticism is called self-conquest, humility, or charity. The false asceticisms—stoicism, Buddhism, spiritism, laicism—all insist upon partial dispositions. They point you toward a closed personality rather than toward an open one as in Christianity. They can as a result turn you aside to morbid and perverse forms of asceticism. But objective and total asceticism is in harmony with normal mental life.

By education you orient and strengthen your mind in order that it may always tend toward its own higher goods easily, freely, and efficiently. To this end you must educate your will.

Re-education of the Will

Those who are abulic (that is, those who suffer loss of will-power) because of not making true acts of the will lose the internal consciousness or feeling for them. *They should above all practice simple acts which are thoroughly willed* (for example, walking, lifting their arm, touching some object) until they recapture the internal feeling of a will act. They should then go on graduating these acts from what is easier to the more difficult.

One young man, though educated in Catholic schools, threw over every moral restraint when he went on to the university. By habitually surrendering to impure vice he ended up in such a state of abulia and indecision that to him it seemed impossible to practice continence. He felt depressed, enslaved, and annihilated in his personality. The vicious obsession was moreover obstructing his concentration in study.

It was not too hard to convince him that by re-educating his will he could remake his personality and recover his onetime vigor. In the first week of treatment he made external acts of the will eight or ten times each day by answering the following questions:

1. *"What's up? When and how is it to be done?"* And he would make a concrete answer: The question is whether or not "to get up out of bed, walk to the right or left," and so forth.

2. *"Is this possible for me? If I order my feet to take me to such and such a position, will they obey me?"* And he got himself to feel the feasibility of this by making affirmative replies. When a somewhat more difficult matter would come up, he would say in a tone of absolute certainty: "Yes, I am sure I can do it!"

3. *"Are there motives for willing this? Yes, even if it be no more than to exercise my personality and educate myself."*

4. *"In that case shall I will it or not? Yes or no?"* And he would make the decision internally, setting aside the contrary possibility.

He experienced so much pleasure at feeling the strength of his will that on the third day he came to tell me all about it. Then he exercised himself in acts that were more difficult and required a greater conquest. Afterward he practiced acts in which his passion was involved; for example, instead of going into such and such a dangerous place, he would go into another. Or he would order his eyes to fix themselves on some inoffensive object instead of an exciting one. And so on.

After sixteen days he was transformed. He had won the fight. He felt himself strong, joyful, and happy. He left all his bad companions. The ideal of scholarship shone anew for him. He recovered ease of concentration. And I should add that to these mental means he added the supernatural one. He also reconciled himself with God in the Sacrament of Penance.

Anyone can use this system to increase his efficiency. All he need do is exercise himself in easy external will acts. Later he should go on to more difficult acts and then to internal acts. For example, you will think about this thing or that. When such and such an idea or fear *comes to you*, decide now to think of or do such and such a certain, definite thing.

Education of the Will by Motives[14]

Your will is a rational faculty, naturally inclined to the good. Before acting, your understanding must precede it like a torchbearer and show it a good, a motive, a value. Then it will move into action. You should, then, propose goods or values to yourself or those whom you are to educate. These values must not only be objectively such but must be comprehended by the subject (that is, by you) as worthwhile at the present moment. In short, they must be objective, subjective, and actual.

Objective values. These are real values, good in themselves; for example, what is useful, honorable, pleasant, necessary. These may be sensory goods perceived by the senses, or spiritual goods grasped by the understanding. They may be goods for time or eternity, partial or total goods, natural or supernatural.

---

[14] See J. Lindworsky, S.J., *Training of the Will*, Milwaukee: Bruce, 1938; and by the same author, *The Psychology of Asceticism*, Westminster, MD: Newman, 1950.

Subjective values. These you perceive to be such. They are accommodated to your capacity. In children, because of their undeveloped understanding, these will be largely sensible goods or those with a sensible element. In adolescents and adults they should also be spiritual and supernatural rather than merely material goods. But they should, as far as possible, be reinforced by the imagination and feelings.

The father of a family once told me, "For a long time I could not succeed in getting my three-year-old son to stop slamming the door. He did not understand the motive (that the noise might bother other people). But one day I gave him another reason which he did understand, 'The door is going to break.' From then on he would neither slam it himself nor let anyone else do so. And he repeated to others the motive as he understood it."

Actual values. They should be actually present in your mind at the moment of decision and execution. To keep them present, it will help to write down your good resolutions and their motives. Then read them over again from time to time. For lack of this continued motivation there are very frequent failures in school and home. Children who went to Mass for years, even daily Mass, sometimes do not go at all later on when they are older. The reason is that they went before not because of any motive of their own, but because of their educators. They did not themselves make an act of the will to go to Mass. In short, the motives were not present when the time came for action.

Education of the Will by Action
In all languages there are two words which are magnificent, ennobling and effective: "yes" and "no." Know how to say

yes when you are going forward with great strides, and also when you are moving on an uphill road, very slowly yet ever onward. Know how to say no without concessions, discussion, or wavering. Herein lies growth and strength.

Active education for those with loss of willpower. If you do not perform true will acts, you will scarcely have any idea of them. What you need above all is an internal experience and intimate feeling of these acts. You must then exercise yourself in external acts which require little effort but are mentally perfect. You must make them concrete, feel their possibility, and produce the mental energy needed for decision.

Active education for all. You will find it very useful to: (1) distinguish true acts of the will from what are not (mere desire, impulse, velleity, or vague intention); (2) make them concrete so as not to be content with a mere desire or plan; (3) pass gradually from the easy to the difficult so as to feel their possibility, avoiding failures (or false acts of the will) and discouragement.

You can also dramatize your will process by considering it as a battle and distinguishing these four stages in it.

1. *Presentation of the contestants:* what are the acts I can will or reject? For instance, shall I stay in bed when I am called or jump out of it?
2. *Struggle between the contestants:* discussion of motives for and against. What good or harm does staying there bring me, and what advantages are there in jumping out?
3. *You can give the victory to whichever one you choose:* feel the possibility of this.
4. *Victory of one over the other:* leave it as master of the field of consciousness. Imagine with concrete

details how you will jump out. Banish the very thought of a possibility of staying in bed (making it impossible for yourself by decision).

The education of the will should not be just a "light-house education" which tries only to avoid shipwrecks on the reefs and shoals of opportunity for evil. Nor should it be a merely negative one which is content to correct defects. Far better will be a positive type of education which will always propose some progress to be attained, perfections to be acquired, virtues to be practiced. This provides an increase of joy, enthusiasm and sense of value. Education lies not so much in making people put what is good into practice as in teaching them to will it and practice it *under their own power.*

I had a student who was really basically good but whose will was very weak and vacillating. He was always being punished. I asked him why he made no effort to correct himself. "I want to, Father, but I can't." I examined his act of will. He did not make it concrete or feel the possibility of it. To help him keep silence at the proper times, I proposed that he bite his tongue (lightly of course) on the way from recreation to study, from study to the classroom or lecture hall. "Can you do that?" "Yes, Father." By making the thing concrete and feeling its possibility he did make definite will acts, one day to please me, another to honor the Blessed Virgin, or to please Our Lord. At night I would ask him, "How many times did you fail?" "Eight." "Then kiss the crucifix eight times and promise not to fail tomorrow." The result was a rapid improvement which was joyful and complete.

The greatest enemy to willpower is the *indecision* common to all such victims. There is a struggle between practical ideas. Shall they act or not? Shall they do this or that? They do not know how to grant victory to one contesting choice and put an end to all discussion by excluding other possibilities. They should be able to correct this quickly.

The Ignatian Method

The noted Dr. Vittoz had a great admiration for St. Ignatius Loyola. He believed that Loyola was three centuries ahead of his time in the fine introspection and effective pedagogy revealed in his *Exercises* and *Examens*. The purpose of St. Ignatius is to make a man perfect. He proceeds according to the most sublime laws of our higher mental activity without allowing the lower levels of activity or disordered feelings to disturb this process. This is indicated in the very first paragraph of his little book.[15] To this end he uses the will's legislative power in the *Exercises* to choose and determine a concrete way of life. In the *Examination of Conscience* (#43) and *Particular Survey* (#24) he uses the will's executive power to bring this down into practice.

The *Exercises* propose motives which are strongest and noblest in themselves and which are reinforced by the feeling of love for Jesus Christ. These motives are to be subjectively felt and adopted by the exercitant. When his higher mental activity has been so directed that passions do not derail it, then come meditations preparatory to the *Art of Christian*

---

[15] "Just as walking, hiking, and running are bodily exercises, so we call spiritual exercises those which prepare and discipline the soul to remove all ill-ordered attachments or hostilities and, once they have been removed, to seek and find the will of God concerning the management of life and one's own role in the Paschal Mystery."—Paragraph #1, *The Spiritual Exercises of St. Ignatius Loyola*, *op. cit.*

Decision-Making (no. 169 ff.). And then come decisions about a way of life and concrete details of the future way of life.

The executive power of the will has a very efficient instrument in the "particular survey."[16] This is truly a control and stimulus to the will. The particular survey has us perform true will acts by making them concrete, each the subject of some one virtue or vice, and in a determined place and time. It makes us feel their possibility and facility by limiting the expenditure of energy and vigilance to a half day at a time. Finally it makes us renew our decision three times a day, and strengthen it by comparison of one time with another, with contrition when we fail and with love of Jesus Christ. It is a *spiritual* treatment which is most efficacious for curing moral illnesses through a *realistic* appraisal and control of personal activity.

Dr. Schleich, a Protestant, professor of the Faculty of Medicine at Berlin, asserts even more. "I say with all assurance and conviction that with these norms and exercises in our hands we could even today transform our asylums, prisons, and mental institutions, and prevent the commitment of two-thirds of the people who are today within their walls."

And so we see that the will is man's conquest of himself, and the education of the will is the strategy of this conquest.

---

[16] *Spiritual Exercises, op. cit.*, paragraphs #24-31.

OUTLINE DIAGRAM

How to Use the Will

Educate the will

- Education necessary
  - We are born incomplete
  - The conflict of our instincts

- Remember for orientation
  - Intense experiences remain
  - Triple scale of values
    - Whole over the part
    - Objective over subjective
    - Development continuous

- By motives
  - Proposed goods to be attained (motives)
  - *Objective* (goods in themselves)
    - Sensible
    - Spiritual
    - Eternal
  - *Subjective* (perceived as such)
    - In childhood first
    - Through the senses
    - Later in the supernatural
  - Actual — actually present
    - When making a decision
    - When carrying it out
    - In continued motivation

- Actively
  - For the abulic
    - Internal experince of will act
    - Practice easy external acts
  - For everyone
    - Distinguish will act from mere desire, impulse, etc.
    - Progress gradually to more difficult acts
    - Dramatize the will process
    - Action under one's own power

- Ignatian method
  - Legislative power of will in the *Exercises*
    - Choice in light of great motives
    - Choice made concrete in Christian Decision-Making
  - Executive power of will in the *particular survey*
    - Concrete
      - Some one virtue or vice in definite place at determined time
    - Possibility felt
      - Half day at a time
      - Renewals of decision thrice daily

9

The Sexual Instinct

Education of the sexual instinct is especially necessary because the lower level of mental activity is antagonistic to the will, is very strong in this matter, and there are very frequent powerful exterior incitements to vice.

Difficulty from an Erroneous Attitude

Many let themselves be mastered by the sexual instinct because they think it irresistible or because they are ignorant of the hidden force of their will, others because of an erroneous persuasion that resistance can cause illness. Very many yield because they expect to find satisfaction in it. They expect to satisfy that thirst for the happiness which all humans seek. However, they seldom reflect upon the transitory and cheap aspect of disordered sex pleasure. It cannot fulfill the noble and unlimited aspirations of the spiritual soul. But they discredit the experience of innumerable people who are physically or mentally sick because of this vice. They count for nothing the testimony of the medical profession, sentences of judges, and warnings of moralists. All of these show the brutal excesses of this instinct once the reins have been loosened by the first concessions.

And on a higher level, they have no suspicion of the deep joys, delicate feelings, mental clearness, and agility of pure souls. They forget the abjection and sadness, despair and emptiness of vice, the tormenting remorse of conscience and the threatened punishment of God.

All education should begin with ideas. When these are modified, then acts are easily corrected. Then by means of acts the feelings and force of the unconscious are controlled.

Is Chastity Possible and Useful for Youth?

If chastity were not possible and useful, no one could will it in earnest, not even if it were imposed merely for social convenience. For the instinct is a brutal one and that barricade very weak. Yet nothing is more contrary to science and experience. The great Jewish psychiatrist of Zurich, Dr. Brueler, affirms, "Whoever recognizes that chastity and continence are possible will hardly have any sexual problems to bother him." Again, the professors of the Faculty of Medicine in Christiania say, "This faculty of medicine has the honor of making the following declaration: The assertion recently put forth by several persons and repeated in newspapers and public gatherings to the effect that a moral life and perfect continence are bad for the health is something that is completely false according to our experience. *We know of no case* of sickness or weakness which we could attribute to perfectly pure and moral conduct."

A document unanimously approved by New York doctors and specialists reads as follows: "In view of the spread of venereal diseases, the results of an unfortunate heredity and the moral evil inseparable from an impure life, we doctors of New York and its environs subscribe unanimously to the declaration *that chastity, a pure life for both sexes, is conformed to the best conditions for physical, moral, and mental health.*" In the Brussels International Conference on Sexual Prophylaxis, 260 members unanimously affirmed the following conclusion: "It is above all necessary to teach male youth that not only are chastity and continence not harmful, but on the contrary these virtues are to be most highly recommended from a purely medical and hygienic point of view." As long ago as its session of March 22, 1917, the Paris Academy of Medicine insisted on the necessity of making known to youth "that chastity is not only possible but also beneficial and to be recommended for health's sake."

Thus we could multiply testimonials from the most eminent doctors of the entire world in order to silence the pseudo-intellectuals or would-be wise men who take pleasure in spreading the opposite idea. And from still another standpoint we know that what God *commands* all men in the Sixth Commandment *cannot* be impossible or harmful to health.

Moreover, the sexual glands, in addition to their external, propagative function, benefit the organism with the production of hormones specific for the sex of the individual. These hormones are necessary for the physiological well-being of the organism.

A Special Difficulty

Acts against purity at a tender age, from six to eleven years, even without knowledge of their malice, frequently throw the lower mental activity out of equilibrium by fixing in the unconscious an abnormal inclination toward pleasure. Or early indulgence may transfer the instinct to the wrong method or sex (sexual inversions), depending on its first realizations. And it leaves a strong tendency to look for comfort, ease, and pleasure in everything, and to flee from a hard life, inconvenience, and pain.

Wrong satisfactions during puberty engrave this emotional pattern even deeper. And it results in an unconscious tendency to reproduce images and memories of pleasure. Persons or circumstances similar to those met in past indulgence at once arouse sexual thoughts or tendencies and impulses to realize them. The environments—movies, beaches, magazines, or pornographic advertising—multiply these incentives until it is extremely difficult to resist passion. This is a difficulty, yes, but not one which it is impossible to conquer.

Remedies

Preventive remedies. Watch over children lest they learn or practice dangerous acts, urged on by bad companions or the example of immoral movies and pictures. But do not see sin where there is none, nor arouse a fear or even the idea of danger or temptation where there is really no moral issue. Else you will be responsible for exaggerated or undue excitability, or an obsessing idea of sex. In the case of adolescents who feel the awakening of instinct and are capable of reflection, teach them in private with dignity and clarity the sublime purpose of Providence in the sexual instinct, the possibility and utility of controlling it, and the grave moral obligation not to go beyond its wise norms. We should calm their nascent curiosity and prevent their satisfying it with corrupt companions. We shall then be able to have them elicit that free-will act without which all will be lost.

Curative remedies. First of all, if erroneous ideas are held, these of course must be corrected.

To counteract the unconscious influence of feelings toward pleasure, arouse contrary feelings and tendencies by accustoming your body to work, a hard life, mortification, and even pain (dignified by Faith), and by withdrawing it from comfort and pleasure. Healthful, vigorous sports are no little aid to this end.

Avoid persons, objects, reading, conversations, and spectacles which involve a less pure association of images and tendencies. To will chastity, yet not avoid these incitements, is like setting out to walk on a slippery hill.

When evil tendencies or thoughts appear resist them at the very first moment, "while they are still weak." Do this by opposing other images (conscious sensations, voluntary concentrations, acts which require attention) and other tendencies (wanting to avoid Hell, win Heaven, please Jesus Christ, save souls).

Whenever one very chaste and virtuous young man met friends and relatives of the other sex, he would be disturbed and attracted by impure thoughts without knowing how to avoid them. It was enough to advise him to practice consciously associating other images with the idea of woman—for instance, the excellence of the mother who bears children for Heaven, the Holy Ghost dwelling within her by grace, the sublimity of the Virgin Mother of God. In a few days he returned to express his gratitude. This new, voluntarily induced association of ideas had done away with the other subconscious and instinctive ones and he felt tranquil and happy.

To attain better resistance avoid lower states of mental activity (alcoholism, romanticism, somnolence, mental vagueness, daydreaming). In these your imagination or subconscious feelings have free rein. And your will and reason are, as it were, asleep. Then the whole man is at the mercy of the first impulse. The first impulse will rise up in a rolling wave, especially if you are also in a too-comfortable bodily position. This latter, because of an unconscious association with the sense of touch, awakens the lowest instincts. You will indeed have the power to resist even then, and for this reason will be responsible for your acts. The holy Curé of Ars fled the sensation of comfort as if it were fire. We should raise the level of this heroic struggle and not make it out to be merely a negative one: "You may not do this; you must avoid that." Rather put it positively as a sacrifice generously offered to our God who has been crucified for us, to love Him, please Him, obey and imitate Him. This positive struggle brings joy and enthusiasm. A negative approach brings only depression.

Against motor ideas which impel you to perform an impure act, oppose the feeling that you are able to avoid it and the concrete will act of an opposite movement. For example, command your feet not to go into a certain place or your hands to remain crossed on your breast for a definite length of time. Do this in order to strengthen your character, develop your personality, please Our Lady, merit Heaven. (Do nothing "in order to avoid sin," for such a reference will awaken the ideas and impulses which you are trying to control.) Made concrete in this way, you can feel these acts as possible and you will really want them.

Once you have done all you humanly can in this very difficult matter, you still need recourse to God to obtain supernatural strength by prayer, confession, and Communion. This grace will never be denied you when you seek it with entire humility, confidence, and perseverance. The experience of many centuries, by all races and men of every intellectual and social position, demonstrates that these supernatural means do conquer the special difficulty of remaining chaste.[17]

---

[17] Cf. the encyclical of Pius XII on Holy Virginity (*Sacra Virginitas*), March 25, 1954; and the encyclical of Pius XI on Christian Marriage (*Casti Connubii*), December 31, 1930.

OUTLINE DIAGRAM

How to Train the Sexual Instinct

Possibility	Testimony: Dr. Brueler Faculty of Medicine of Christiania Doctors of New York and environs International Conference at Brussels Paris Academy of Medicine God commands it		
Difficulty	Fixation of inclination toward pleasure because of acts performed Association of ideas and tendencies		
Remedy	Preventive	Watch over children Instruct adolescents Stress acts of the will	
	Curative	Correct erroneous ideas Form positive tendencies and contrary habits Avoid incentives	
		Resist beginnings with	other images other tendencies
		Avoid states of lower mental activity	
		Oppose bad impulses with	concrete will acts the conviction of triumph
		Prayer, Confession, Communion	

10

Feelings

Feeling is a force God gives you for willing and working with greater energy and constancy. But, like steam in a locomotive, it is a chaotic force. If well channeled by reason (with its safety valves and opportune expansion and release), it will be exceedingly useful to you.

General Control
Do Not Let Feelings Govern You

Make no change under the influence of feelings. To have as a norm of action "because I like to" is the same as to take a trolley car or bus without bothering about where it is going or only because it is more comfortable or is shinier than another. Likewise, to stop working "because it is a bother" or "troublesome" is to renounce success, joy, glory, and even your own salvation.

> *To want something only because there is no other way out is the way a slave acts.*

> *To want it because it is no trouble (following likes or impulses) is the way an animal acts.*

To want it in spite of the bother (guided by reason or duty) is the way a rational human being acts.

To want even the bother of it (with your eyes on the ideal or on God) is the way a hero or saint acts.

The child and the socially maladapted person love or hate, work or stop working, only because of their likes and dislikes, because reason has not been developed or has been inhibited.

Govern Your Feelings

Restrain exaggeration of feelings. Do not give too much importance to them, or to what pleases or displeases you, or to what you fear or desire. For experience tells us that feeling heightens colors, exaggerates good or evil, obscures and alters truth.

For example, do the words or behavior of another irritate you? Then your feelings will make you tend to think that he has a deliberate bad intention (whereas he probably acted only out of light-mindedness or without full reflection). They will even persuade you that he has yet worse plans for the future. Does the mailman or telegraph messenger bring you bad news? At least your imagination will immediately run riot and overload the unopened envelope with the blackest shadows. "Somebody is dead," you may think. Or, "Some relative has gone bankrupt." Do you feel a little unwell? Your uncontrolled thought will tell you, "It must be tuberculosis, or heart trouble, or the beginnings of insanity." Is it a case of not making progress in your studies, or in virtue, or prayer? Do you find yourself sad and discouraged and wish to give up the spiritual life you adopted? Does it seem to you that you were not made for this? In all these cases you have lost control of your feelings *by letting them become exaggerated*. Convince yourself that the real situation is much better than your emotional reaction to it.

Control Your Thoughts

Do not give free rein to their deceptive arguments. Avoid their exaggerations and transfers to other fields. Think about something else and, above all, *do not change your plans or make important resolutions* under the sway of feeling. Let a day go by. Let a night go by, too. "Consult your pillow." Then, when your feelings are calmed, you will be disposed for work and you will see that "the lion is not so fierce as he is painted." With regard to mental illness as a dreaded possibility one must discount fear; believe psychiatrists when they say that those who become demented were the ones who had no fear of becoming so.

With his fine sense of psychology St. Ignatius traces out for us three very wise rules for governing ourselves when a depressing feeling comes over us.

Firstly, in time of desolation (that is, when you are discouraged or sad, without light or strength, without peace or consolation, or when temptation blinds you) make no change, but continue with the plans you made when you had peace, light, and consolation.

Secondly, think of the fact that this state will pass and that light and joy will return. Encourage the thoughts and feelings you had before the desolation came.

Thirdly, act against the very desolation. Do the opposite of what you feel yourself inclined to do. Lengthen your prayer, for example, or perform even more mortifications.

In the Palace of Feelings there are brilliant halls where dwell optimism, hope, love, valor, and joy. And there are dark cellars, lurking places of discouragement, sadness, fear, worry, anger. The mistress of the Palace, the will, has to pass through all its rooms but can delay wherever she wishes. We should not give too much importance to fears or sadness when they come. We should not habitually and voluntarily stay with them, but pass on to the halls of joy and optimism.

Open the Safety Valve

There are states of feeling in which repression can cause fatigue, suffering, and illness. Such are the apparent conflicts between the commands of duty and the demands of honor, love, or instinct. Frequently the mere manifestation of these to your mental guide or spiritual director will lighten them, reveal the solution, and cure them.

During the First World War psychiatrists were surprised to note the greater number of cases of severe mental illness among English soldiers than among the French. They investigated the causes and found that the former had been brought up in the atmosphere of believing that an Englishman should not feel fear and that it would be a national disgrace to give any sign of it. This mentality imposed on many individuals a violent struggle, repression of unavoidable feelings, and finally mental disequilibrium. When this mentality was modified, there were fewer victims.

There are four kinds of difficulties or internal conflicts which we should make known as soon as possible to a prudent director lest they poison our wills or at least tire our minds unnecessarily.

1. *Acts* that weigh down our conscience with moral responsibility.
2. *Worrisome practical doubts* that we cannot solve, or obsessing temptations to evil.
3. *Tormenting indecision* in important matters (this may be a result of the preceding).
4. *Oppressing fears or sadness* that we do not know how to control.

When a tumor is opened, the victim is relieved. So a release of these emotional conflicts with a prudent friend or spiritual guide and, above all, the divine release of them in sacramental Confession, roots out of our soul all that poisonous overload. It brings us so much peace, joy, and encouragement that non-Catholic doctors of different countries agree that if Confession had not been established in the Church as a spiritual medicine, they would have had to prescribe it themselves as a treatment for emotional ailments rising from disordered feelings.

You should also open the safety valve of dignified affection in the expansions of family love, true friendship, spiritual confidences, love of your neighbor, love of souls, and love of God. All your mental energy does not flow into the channel of your understanding when you try to close off or block up the channel of feeling. There must be some release of feeling.

Close the Escape Valve to Brute Instinct and Disordered Passions

A fourth-year medical student once came to see me after a lecture. He could not sleep, study, or fix his attention. He was wallowing in discouragement, depression, and profound sadness. He had to stop attending classes. He had been studying intensely, at the same time had to attend to troublesome family affairs, and was also worrying about an illness of his father's. He consulted an atheistic psychiatrist who recommended certain injections and that he give vent to his sexual instinct. This latter, according to the diagnosis, was being repressed and was the cause of his illness. The young man followed this foolish advice only to find himself even more confused, sad, and worried. Once the true cause of his sickness was found and all was made right with God through Confession, he began the work of re-education joyfully. He recovered his ability to sleep in two days.

Apparently there are not a few atheistic psychiatrists who follow Freud (as they say) and want to re-establish lost equilibrium by subjecting the angel to the brute, the soul to the body, the higher mental activities to the lower, the conscious to the unconscious. Dr. Vittoz and his whole school, together with all spiritual psychiatrists, are in revolt against such an aberration.

You should also do away with useless confidences which are born of emotionalism or impulse. Never recount to any person you meet, just to console yourself, what you suffer or fear, desire or plan. This might give you some momentary consolation (that of yielding to the impulse), but the sad ideas will impress you more in the telling and make you more their slave. If you tell them to your friends, you make them sad; if to your enemies, you make them glad. The ills of another, and much less the details of what you suffer, feel, or fear, are not of much interest to anyone even though his charity or courtesy lead you to think so. On the other hand, if you forget yourself in the affairs of other people, you will at the same time get your own feelings under control, learn something useful, and acquire an affable and sympathetic personality.

11

The Power of Wrath

"If you have an enemy," says Dr. Fosdick, "or dislike someone, the greatest evil you can do, not to him but yourself, is to allow hatred to sink into your soul and plough a lasting furrow there."

To control the emotion of anger it will be helpful to know its psycho-physiological trajectory. Here we shall diagram only its controllable or voluntary phase, referring the reader to chapter 5 for the diagram of the first or spontaneous phase. Here we are using *anger* as a concrete illustration of the growth and flowering of emotions and feelings.

A. Spontaneous Phase

Injustice, insults, or annoyances affect the cerebral cortex by means of the senses or imagination. If we perceive these as contrary to our life, honor, health, or ideals, we form one of the three following judgments.

"I, They, It"

I: "With my good qualities, merits, and intentions, I do not deserve such treatment."

They: "They are unfair, cruel, ungrateful, or unbearable."

It: "It [the event] is unfair, unjust, intolerable, dangerous."

Especially if it is very prolonged and is felt to be very strong, this concrete judgment stimulates the hypothalamus which is the engine room of the emotions. Thence the autonomic nervous system spontaneously goes into action. This, plus the action of adrenaline, puts heart, stomach, lungs, muscles, viscera, etc., in hyperactivity. And we are invaded by feelings of disgust and antipathy.

This is an example of what the classical moral philosophers and moral theologians call *motus primo primi*. In it there is no responsibility nor any sin. We really cannot control it except indirectly, and then only with a great deal of vigilance. We can try to avoid the exciting factor, or at least the memory of it, and to shorten its duration. We do find that we are able to avoid making the concrete judgment, "I, They, It," or at least to modify it once it is present in us. This we can do either by deliberately interposing a distraction or, better, by deliberately forming in ourselves a different attitude by means of an adequate education or re-education. If we do this, the disturbance will pass rather quickly without leaving behind a lasting or profound effect.

B. *Voluntary Phase*

I. Destructive Development

These disturbances in the organs themselves affect the cerebral cortex and warn us that we are beginning to be annoyed. The original stimulus itself may also be continuing to solicit our emotions. If the will, which could have distracted our attention to other things, gives in to anger, we shall retain the concrete judgment, "I, They, It." This judgment will become stronger and more prolonged and will prepare us for attack or some other reaction.

The reaction may be wholly unrestrained, in which case the hypothalamus will develop an *animal wrath* or unrestrained anger with primitive animal reactions. Or perhaps, faced with social conventions or fear of reprisals, we shall be content with a restrained attack, that is to say, with a corroding *impatience* which will be accompanied by threats, or by acts which annoy our adversary, or by a feeling of disgust or sadness. Or, finally, we may resolve to postpone the attack, on which occasion we conceive *hatred* or "bottled wrath" together with tension and prolonged inner disturbances.

In all of these three states the organism calls all its reserves into battle: the overexcited autonomic nervous system, the adrenaline which flows in the bloodstream and activates all the organs, the pituitary gland which liberates the hormone ACTH. This latter stimulates the suprarenal glands where there are manufactured what we might call the atomic bombs of the organism, i.e., the groups of hormones which affect mineral metabolism, gluco-metabolism, and androgen. All these help to produce a revolution or overexcitation which is more sustained than that of the nervous system, but which liberates an enormous amount of energy as if for use in an emergency.

Moreover, the medulla of the suprarenal glands produces adrenaline which then stimulates even more the hypothalamus and the pituitary gland. Then we begin to feel the effects of hypertension in the circulatory system and musculature, the heart pounds, and the lungs labor as if to obtain more oxygen. The stomach contracts, thus stopping or disturbing the process of digestion. The whole organism becomes poisoned if anger is prolonged, and then fatigue and disgust invade us. After the emotion has passed, our resistance is weakened

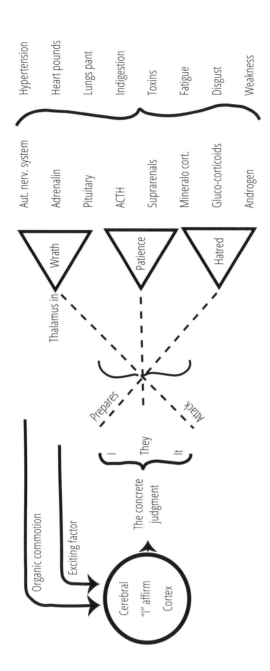

I-Destructive

Hypertension
Heart pounds
Lungs pant
Indigestion
Toxins
Fatigue
Disgust
Weakness

Aut. nerv. system
Adrenalin
Pituitary
ACTH
Suprarenals
Mineralo cort.
Gluco-corticoids
Androgen

Wrath
Patience
Hatred

Thalamus in

Prepares
Attack

I They It

The concrete judgment

Organic commotion
Exciting factor

Cerebral "I" affirm Cortex

Figure 9

and we become depressed at feeling ourselves conquered by the emotion. Sometimes, too, there may come upon us an unholy joy at seeing an adversary suffer. But all these evils can be avoided by controlling the concrete judgment and by making anger subordinate to reason rather than to passion. Otherwise there are results such as in a New Orleans clinic where 76 percent of the patients were found to be there because of anger, hatred, or impatience, mixed with fear or anxiety.

II. *Victorious Development*

When the signals of an emotional disturbance come to the cerebral cortex, we notice that we are becoming annoyed and that our organism is beginning to prepare itself for attack or defense. The stimulus itself, the injury or the memory of one, may still be exciting us also. Then, instead of letting ourselves be dominated by the emotion, if we order that it be controlled, the free will can follow either or both of two procedures.

First, it can modify the concrete judgment, "I, They, It," either by weakening it through a distraction or, better, annihilating it by a contrary judgment.

Secondly, it can order the contrary internal attitude of love and sympathy and the external expression of this on the face, in the tone of voice, and in muscular activity.

Control by means of distraction.
"Every morning," says the Doctor of Gentleness, St. Francis de Sales, "prepare your soul for a tranquil day." When you are at peace, foster this advantageous state for the sake of your own advancement. Continually exercise yourself in acts of

goodness and gentleness. If something bothers you, do not be disturbed or resist it. But when it comes, humble yourself graciously in the presence of God and try to put your soul into a tranquil state. Say, "Yes, I stumbled there; I must be more careful." Do this always, however often you fail. Wait, have patience, gather your forces, and you will win the spirit of peace and gentleness.

We have often heard this advice given: "Calm down, don't answer, control yourself, have patience." It would be more effective if, instead of wanting to remove the feeling (which is an effect of ideas), we were to remove or modify the ideas which cause it. When another insults you or his conduct disgusts you, instead of thinking about the injustice or grossness of his behavior, concentrate your attention on something else—objects or colors before you, or the sound waves coming at you from all directions, or (if you are a psychologist) in observing his waste of energy, his attitudes and reactions. You would then feel hardly any commotion.

Control by means of the contrary idea.
1. Discover which of the three, "I, They, It," predominates in you and formulate the contrary of it.

2. To the thought of pride or fear which the emotion arouses, e.g., "I do not deserve this treatment," oppose the following: "I am a man like others, with limitations, defects, and transgressions which would deserve a greater punishment."

Instead of the idea that "They are unjust or cruel," insist on what experience teaches, namely that "Everyone has lesser defects and greater virtues than we tend to admit when we are angry." Or, "They must have done that without thinking of what they were doing, or at least there was no bad will there."

II-Victorious

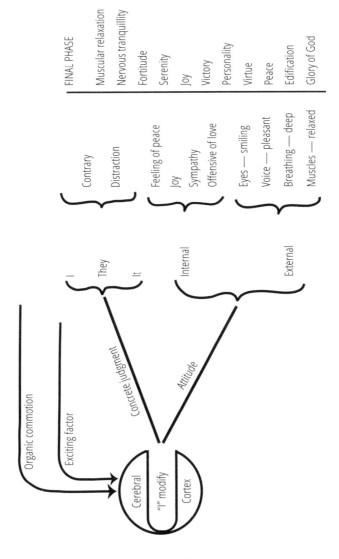

FINAL PHASE
Muscular relaxation
Nervous tranquillity
Fortitude
Serenity
Joy
Victory
Personality
Virtue
Peace
Edification
Glory of God

Contrary
Distraction

Feeling of peace
Joy
Sympathy
Offensive of love

Eyes — smiling
Voice — pleasant
Breathing — deep
Muscles — relaxed

I
They
It

Internal

External

Concrete judgment

Attitude

Organic commotion

Exciting factor

Cerebral
"I" modify
Cortex

Figure 10

Jesus Christ on the Cross used this means when He asked pardon for those who crucified and insulted Him, saying that their guilt was less because "they know not what they do."

3. If you are a spiritual man, a Christian with a living faith, reflect that an insult is what you deserve because of your sins. Think that it is a great opportunity offered you by God to gain by a minute's patience and humiliation "an eternal reward of glory."

A Sister of Charity was once begging alms for her orphans. "An alms?" answered an anticlerical man, "to support you in idleness and help enslave those kids? This is what you need." And he struck her. The sister thought for a moment about her sins and replied without a change of countenance, "That was for me, sir. Now, something for my orphans." The man's anger vanished; he asked her pardon and gave her a substantial donation.

If the mere presence of that good person for whom you have an aversion draws a curl to your lip and brings you a thousand sharp thoughts and words, do a bit of spiritual gymnastics and meditate on his virtues. See in him "Jesus Christ disguised in his defects," who draws near to you that you may smile on Him, love Him, speak to Him, and serve Him with greater merit. Our Divine Master said, "As long as you did it for one of these, the least of my brethren, you did it for Me."

4. Finally, the event itself, the "It," is not too unbearable nor too dangerous. If it deprives us of some earthly good, or convenience, or comfort, yet this and all the goods of the world are no more than an insignificant speck of dust in comparison with the everlasting goods which are prepared as the reward

of our suffering. "Although it be encircled with thorns, it is a diamond for heaven." Injury or insult is an incendiary explosion which can be triggered and detonated only by our thoughts of protest. (At the end of chapter 14 you will find some examples of thoughts for changing sorrow into joy.)

Control by means of the contrary feeling.
We must try to substitute feelings of joy, peace, and sympathy for the feeling of disgust, perturbation, or antipathy which our emotions would tend to arouse in us. Above all we must digest inevitable suffering by accepting it fully, if we wish it not to go on poisoning us. We must treat persons *as if* they were very congenial and sympathetic. We must try to understand and value their virtues and excuse their defects. We must use a tone of respectful affection, pay them deference and do them services, pray and sacrifice for them. A month of this treatment will be enough to make us congenial and sympathetic ourselves. For knowing how to think well of others and how to smile on them is the secret of multiplying friends.

Bandits once attacked the house of a colleague of mine in China. He received their chiefs with all courtesy and kindness, just as he would orderly and more advanced people. He invited them to tea, candy, and cigarettes in his reception room. When he brought them to the door, they met others of the bandits making off with the missionary's mules. The chiefs ordered them returned and went away without doing any harm whatever.

Control by means of the contrary expression.
We should also use the method which is more physiological. Our voice, breathing, eyes and muscles should be given an expression contrary to that which anger would impose upon

us. We should either remain silent or at least speak deliberately, quietly, and pleasantly. If a cry of hatred or impatience is about to escape through your mouth, breathe deeply two or three times and release the air slowly, and you will extinguish it. Keep the muscles of arms and hands, mouth and face loose and relaxed. Above all make sure that a smile gives the eyes a kindly, gentle expression. And at the same time keep your thoughts on something pleasant.

After one of my lectures in Rio de Janeiro a lady came up to tell me about her troubles, her bad temper, and that of her husband. "My home is a hell," she said. "We are always quarreling, although we pass for good Christians, and even devout ones." I advised that she go look at herself in a mirror and practice smiling with her eyes. "When you have learned how to make this deep and open smile, and when you know that your husband is returning home, make an act of Faith: 'Here comes Jesus Christ disguised in the defects of my husband. He is coming so that I may smile at Him, love Him, and serve Him.'" A month later she came back to thank me for the advice; her home had been transformed. They were happy. She had modified the thought and the external expression of anger.

12

Fear

Could we succeed in banishing exaggerated insecurity and fear from the earth, we would double the health and happiness of the human race.

As children, says Fosdick, we feared only two things: falling down and loud noises. After passing through the fears of childhood, experience teaches us that many fears are groundless. And we protect ourselves against unreasonable fears. Yet oftentimes the environment and our imagination lead us to see dangers where there are really none. Or they may magnify our fears a hundredfold.

Strong impressions of terror or lively bouts of anxiety and fear, whether they come from conversation, or from a vivid imagination, or the movies, leave something like a residue or sedimentation in the subconscious. This residue is a tendency toward insecurity or a feeling of anxiety. And when this feeling invades an idle mind, it tends to fill it with anxious images, provoking organic alterations such as physical inhibitions, trembling, contraction of the blood vessels, pallor, panting for breath, palpitations, and so forth. Fear is a monster which dwells in the caverns of the subconscious. The more vague and confused it is, the more it afflicts us. We should drag it out from its hidden lair, look at it face-to-face, and then we shall destroy it.

Degrees of Fear

We said in the first part that the idea or apprehension of "danger," whether real or imaginary, is the cause of fear. Fear and its consequent inhibitions keep on increasing in proportion to the magnitude of the danger, its proximity, and the difficulty of avoiding it. So at the mere possibility of a misfortune or because of an imagined inability to cope with it, our physical movements and our very speech lose their spontaneity. When we merely walk out in front of a large audience, all of whom have their eyes on us, very few of us will even walk naturally. If our lack of confidence turns into alarm at a really probable or great danger, the unity of our wishing, thinking, and acting is broken, and even our muscles tremble. We are literally "shaken up," and if the serious danger or misfortune seems to be *inevitable,* then anxiety tends to destroy all control of movements, ideas, and emotions. Even the memory can be inhibited, as when timid students take examinations.

Finally, if the fear goes a step further and the danger seems to be imminent, serious, and inevitable, panic can take hold of us and bring anarchy into our thoughts, feelings, and actions. Paralysis of all our powers may follow if the fear is extremely great. An example of this is the confusion and witless panic that often come with an earthquake or a fire in a theater.

How to Control Fear

Fear is the emotion most difficult to control because often we do not know what we fear or why we are afraid, as in cases of anxiety, phobias, or groundless fears. The motive is often unconscious or may be transferred from its real cause to some accompanying circumstance. Or we may be unconsciously repressing some natural reaction which might humiliate us, we think, if seen.

Instead, we give it expression in "symbolic" fears which we recognize as groundless, but which we do not know how to control. In such cases a deeper exploration of the subconscious is indicated, an investigation of the abnormality and the circumstances which first accompanied it. Discovering these, we may more easily control a transferred fear.

If the fear is *conscious*, we may take the following steps to conquer it:

1. *Before all else, act.* Fear already tends to inhibit our activities. So we must not assist it by remaining inactive but, on the contrary, conquer it by acting. A North Pole explorer owes his rescue to such a procedure. Lost on the endless ice, he could not find his camp. Instead of worrying about it, he began to heap up piles of snow and ice at regular intervals. These helped him to make calculations through which he eventually rediscovered his camp.

2. *Make them concrete.* We must illuminate those dark caverns. Answer these questions in writing and in detail: "Just what am I afraid of? And why?" When fear or anxiety is made concrete and viewed objectively, it is destroyed.

3. *Reason about them.* "What probabilities are there that this [the thing I fear] will really happen? And even if it does happen, will it really be as disastrous as I fear?"

4. *Face up to them.* "Even supposing that this happens, what then? So what? Are there not others who have gone through

similar crises? Haven't they gone on living and become happy? And even if I have to die, so what? Then can't I begin to be happier in eternity?"

When we imagine the worst possible natural evil that could happen to us and sincerely accept it and so find a human or divine solution for it, we shall be victorious over exaggerated fear.

5. *Avoid the exciting factors, or rather the alarming ideas, which these stimuli arouse in us.* Distract your attention from them by means of concentrating it upon conscious sensations or by deliberately following out a favorite train of thought or, even better—

6. *Deliberately affirm contrary judgments,* e.g., "There is no special danger. The probability that this will happen is very small. Even if it does happen, the disadvantage would be insignificant, or at least there would come with it several advantages which would far counterbalance it."

7. *Deliberately foster contrary feelings,* e.g., of courage, or security. This is done by the same means by which fear betrayed us, i.e., by intense acts of courage, by vivid remembrances of peaceful moments or places, by actually saying something with a tone of courage or security in the voice.

8. *Associate this reliving of past peaceful moments with the circumstances which had been producing anxiety in you.* Imagine that you are in control of the situation and that you are speaking in a masterful tone of voice such as in the case of the young man with the pills or the patient with the locust (chapter 5).

In a Brazilian seminary I met a stammerer who was afraid that he would be unable to go on to the priesthood because of this defect. Face-to-face with the rector of the seminary he could not speak two consecutive words. The same thing would happen when with certain of his companions and in certain classes. On the contrary he spoke well whenever he had learned something by memory. Hence it was the feeling of anxiety which was inhibiting his vocal muscles. He was afraid that the rector would declare him unsuitable for the priesthood. But I helped him to remove this fear by showing him that he could cure himself if he would implant the contrary feelings in his subconscious by the means indicated above. And so I had him link these feelings to the experience which had terrified him most. I had him imagine and then actually say, "I am going to see Father Rector ... I greet him ... And all is serene. I am completely at peace and am master of the situation." At first he spoke the last phrase with the same descriptive tone as the first. But I had him repeat it after me with a tone of security. On doing it with all the courage and force of which he was capable, I felt that he was transformed. Three days later the rector came to thank me for the good done to his seminarians, and he particularly mentioned that the stammerer had been cured.

9. *In cases of muscular constriction, try to loosen the muscles.* By this I mean a latent state of insecurity or anxiety due to strong and prolonged tension in the intercostal muscles. This prevents the quiet easy expansion of the chest which is normal when we are secure or in good spirits. Instead, we would then tend to assume a posture characteristic of timidity or depression. But, since there appear to be no mental or emotional causes of fear, we should try to loosen these muscles by adequate gymnastic exercises, a more correct posture, or massage.

10. *Assume the opposite facial expression:* not the wide-open, staring eyes which are a sign of fear, but rather a look that is secure and mild. Keep the voice deep and firm; let it rely on the outgoing air current and not on forcing the throat muscles. Maintain a respiration that is deeper or slower. To do this, instead of concentrating on expanding the lungs, try to expand the nasal passages and keep them well opened.

How to Control Scruples

The obsessing insecurity of scruples can find expression in profane matters, as in the case of one who goes out of his house and is worried whether he put out the lights, turned off the faucet, or locked the door. This kind of obsession also, and frequently, finds expression in religious or moral affairs. A religious scruple is a torturing but unfounded fear of sinning or having sinned. It is an error or anguishing doubt caused by a strong fear which inhibits or disturbs the reason. Scruples are the source of anxiety or sadness, of many organic ailments, bashfulness, and many personality disturbances. If not controlled in time, scruples can become the occasion of despair, moral relapses, and even moral perversion.

The predisposing causes of scruples are the same as those indicated above for exaggerated impressionability or exaggerated emotions in general, such as organic weakness and nervous exhaustion. Another cause is a temperament that tends to look upon the negative side of things. Or it may be one or more of the following: a residue of insecurity because of not having taken action against previous unreasonable fears, an uncontrolled and exaggerated imagination, an excessively strict education, much dealing with scrupulous people, an anxious desire for excessive certitude, or fear of responsibility.

A scruple may also be a temptation of the devil. When it is very prolonged, it is almost always an indication of psychoneurosis and sometimes of psychosis. In other words, a scruple can be one of many symptoms of mental illness, but of itself it does not indicate an evil moral life or lack of faith.

Remedies for Scruples

1. Before all else make sure that it is really a scruple and not merely ignorance or a passing test prompted by God. This judgment should be made by the director or adviser and not by the person himself.

2. Then admit what is scientifically proven, that is, that scruples are a mental and not a moral illness. He should recall what we said about the "degrees of fear." Whenever the fear is great (and there is no greater fear than that caused by the idea of eternal damnation), this not only inhibits and disturbs his muscles, but also his mind and feelings. The emotion of fear is so disturbing to the scrupulous person that it makes him see danger where there is none or see grave sin where there is only an imperfection or a venial fault.

3. Fight the battle on the proper terrain. Do not pretend to destroy this mental *and natural* enemy with means that are spiritual or supernatural such as absolution. What should we say to someone who comes up to a priest and keeps saying, "Father save me. I have such a toothache I know I am going to hell." The answer should be: "Go see a dentist, but do not think you are lost because of a reason like that." The scrupulous person must be told something similar. "Do not give an eternal dimension to what is only an emotional disturbance."

4. Recognize, then, that emotion *disturbs the judgment* so much that it makes one see what does not exist. This often happens when timid persons think they see apparitions at night. They forget it when they discover the phantasm, or appearance, is really something that they know very well. But they run away in terror if the fear gets control of them. Once upon a time there was a blind man, led along by a guide, who all of a sudden stopped and said, "I can't go another step; I *see* a deep pit in front of me." Of course, being blind, he could not see what was really not there, but he had something in his imagination. Something like this happens in the case of the scrupulous man when, despite his confessor's judgment, he sees sin and sacrilege in receiving Communion. We should insist that he receive Communion, but, instead of losing time examining his conscience over and over again and weighing the "sacrilege" that he thinks he sees, he should repeat acts of love and confidence. Such faith and obedience, which relinquish one's own judgment for God's sake, are heroic. And each such act of love itself gives or increases grace.

5. Whoever had a clock or thermometer out of order would be advised by everyone not to be guided by it, but to follow normal clocks or thermometers. So, God gives a right to the scrupulous person not to be guided or changed by what his disturbed conscience tells him, but by what his director tells him. More than this, his Heavenly Father asks him to use this right, to lay aside for a time his subjective judgment, and to remain at peace.

6. When the scruple is concerned with one's past life, even despite a series of general confessions; when a person thinks that he has forgotten or has not confessed well, or that his

confessors have not understood him, he should remember that by means of indirect absolution all his sins have already been forgiven on the day on which he made a confession with good will. The obligation of making known forgotten sins in a subsequent confession pertains only to those which are certainly mortal, certainly committed, and certainly omitted from confession. And even this obligation ceases for a scrupulous person.

7. Many confuse the concepts of perfect confession and good confession. An absolutely perfect confession could be made only by God who knows perfectly the responsibility of every act. We can all make at least a good confession, for this demands only good will on our part. Many scrupulous people could hardly do any more than this because of the blocks in their minds and their disturbed emotions. They should realize, then, that in such a good confession, absolution directly pertains to the sins of which they accuse themselves, and indirectly pertains to those which they have forgotten or those of which they did not accuse themselves perfectly, although they acted with good will at the time of the confession.

More than this, when their nervousness and confused ideas about the examination of conscience and confession itself begin to torture them, we must remember what moral theology teaches us. If the integrity of Confession would tend to do them serious psychical harm, then with their confessor's approval, they may content themselves with a general accusation or merely ask for absolution, renewing their contrition for all their past sins.

Instead of worrying about past confessions, they should increase their faith in Christ who washes all sins away through

His Most Precious Blood. They should trust in the infinite mercy which delights in pardon and is shown to us in the parable of the Prodigal Son.

8. In the case of scrupulous people who are obsessed with doubts concerning internal acts, such as their thoughts, desires, intentions, feelings, sorrow, or purpose of amendment, they should be forbidden not only to accuse themselves, but even to examine themselves in this regard. For if it is difficult for all of us to measure our responsibility for such internal acts, for the scrupulous person it is impossible. The scrupulous person is often concerned about his "thoughts." So he must be told that thoughts, of themselves, are not sins. To be sinful the thought, for instance, of a forbidden pleasure would have to be deliberately *chosen by the will.* And one would have to want the thought with the intention of gaining the forbidden pleasure, relishing the thought somewhat as one who chews a caramel.

9. Since the scrupulous person is scarcely living at all in the present and does not take exact account of what he sees and hears but is always wrapped up in his subjective thoughts, he should work to increase his conscious life with voluntary sensations by "living in the present" or by practicing the "Do what you are doing." (See chapter 3.)

10. He should also re-educate his power of concentration by accustoming himself to think about only one thing at a time. The scrupulous man does not know how to detach himself from his obsession whenever he is studying, conversing, or walking.

11. Above all, he should strengthen his will by repeated acts of decision and by assuming responsibilities. These activities

have in his case been almost extinguished. To this end the director should not always take upon himself the responsibility for decisions, but, little by little, should bring it about that the person suffering from scruples take this responsibility upon himself.

After a lecture a lady came to see me. She had been suffering for seventeen years from persistent scruples. These had stolen away all her peace and joy. She could not go to Communion unless Confession had immediately preceded it. Even then she went in fear and trembling. She seemed quite discouraged and in a decline. I proved to her that her illness was not moral but psychic. I managed to convince her that she had nothing to fear for her soul, but that her health was in danger. I explained that the working of a scruple was not intellectual but emotional. For example, there were one or more frightful experiences or thoughts establishing this feeling in the unconscious. From this unconscious level they bothered her by arousing fear of sin, either when similar images or happenings occurred or when she had similar depressing feelings.

I explained to her the conditions for mortal sin: full consciousness and a deliberate act of the will in a serious matter. These conditions were, of course, not verified in her case. By thus eliminating the root of fear she could promise herself that in the future she would not fear the scruple but discredit it. She would substitute a conscious sensation for it whenever it arose. By means of conscious acts, each time repeated more frequently, she began to come out of her merely subjective world and live in the objective order. She was cured by the time she had come for two interviews. When I saw her again six months later, she was healthy, joyful, and happy.

The scruples returned only once, during a mental crisis occasioned by the death of her father. But she mastered them in a very short time.

12. He should exact of himself blind obedience to his director, an obedience which is founded upon supernatural faith. He should recognize that he is blind, that he needs a guide, and that for the time being he has a right not to be guided by or make changes in accordance with what his disturbed conscience tells him. He should follow what his director says to do. And in moments of doubt he must adhere to what has been determined or resolved upon at a more tranquil time or with the director's aid.

13. He should not be moved by doubts or a "perhaps," but only by evidence, and he should faithfully observe the following three rules:
   a. Never to accuse himself of doubts or temptations concerning the matter about which (his director has advised him) he is scrupulous.
   b. Not to review or talk about his past confessions or sins of his past life.
   c. While going about his everyday business, not to give any importance to sudden doubts.

He must accept the fact that his illness has been derived from throwing himself into action while in a state of doubt, and that it is an illness which is valuable experience for him because it helps him to get control of his anxiety and get closer to a normal state. He must accept the fact that every time he tries to obtain any momentary alleviation of his trouble by means of giving in to his tendency to doubt, such an occasion will be a prologue to greater troubles.

14. He should be content with human security about salvation or the state of grace. He should not desire to have the kind of security or certitude proper to God's knowledge or that of men who are in heaven (the kind that excludes all possibility of the opposite). Thus, he will help to bring about that state of confidence which is so pleasing to God.

15. He should increase this confidence by repeated concrete acts, even if the effort to overcome the contrary feeling calls for heroism on his part.

16. He should fight against the unconscious feeling of fear or doubt which is the remote root of scruples. He should frequently repeat thoughts, sentences, and acts of courage and confidence.

Recall the case of St. Francis de Sales for whom an intense and prolonged expression of love was the adequate counterweight and cure for a tendency to scrupulosity.

17. Change the negative attitude of a person who fears and trembles at sin and personal responsibility for a different, positive attitude which concentrates on and examines how he might have pleased God more, aided his neighbor more effectively, or practiced virtue in a better way. He should shift the direction of his thoughts and self-examination from sins to the virtues.

18. Finally, he should relax the tensions in his muscles and practice breathing more slowly, rhythmically, and deeply. Especially should he practice relaxation of eyes and forehead. He should wear a smile on his face like one who knows that his fears were exaggerated and due to an illness rather than being any real danger to his soul.

Feelings of Inferiority

What begins as timidity or cowardice can degenerate into a feeling of inferiority or an "inferiority complex." This may be due to there having been little or no expression of security or of one's own personality during infancy or adolescence. Perhaps his education was excessively protective and warded off from him every exposure to difficulty or danger. This would likely result in an inability to overcome difficulty or danger. Or perhaps other people always made the decisions for him, and he never became accustomed to assuming responsibility himself. Or it may have been due to a frequent experience of fear which was not counteracted at once by positive thoughts. Then the fear remained at a subconscious level in the same manner as insecurity or a tendency to be upset (like one who is easily "shaken up" or easily "thrown off balance").

Or all this may come from a *false concept of inferiority* because of some past failure, the importance and consequences of which his wounded self-love multiplies a hundredfold. Or his timidity may be grounded upon some *real* defect or a *real* incapacity in one particular field, which his imagination *extends* to other areas while hiding away his real talents and good qualities.

It may even be due to an *excessive ambition* or to the kind of depression that results from seeking unrealistic goals. Or he may be a man seeking merely human success without giving importance to success in the eyes of God. In other words, whoever in all his actions seeks and delights in realizing the will of God, the ideal of Infinite Wisdom, by this alone can feel full satisfaction even though human success fails him. For God's highest plans may include human failure without impeding His glory. God obtains what He desires not by our action but through our sanctification, humiliation, or other supernatural means.

Sometimes this feeling of inferiority may come from an *irrational panic* about "what they will say" or fear of ridicule. Timidity is in direct proportion to our desire not to be criticized. Hence the capacity to laugh at oneself and at everything laughable counteracts timidity. Laughter is the secret of good humor, a fountain of health, and a condition of our acceptance in society.

A sense of inferiority is sometimes the result of *comparing oneself to others*. This is especially liable to happen if a person is involved with others who are better prepared or highly talented. In such a situation think of the fact that everyone has his own good qualities and aptitudes from God and that he will give an account of them to God. Remember that the man who received ten talents and gained ten others was not more highly praised than the man who received one talent and gained one more. You must develop your own personality—"Be yourself!"—and not try to be a "rubber stamp" of anyone else. The grandeur of man is not in physical appearance but in moral value. Oftentimes a noble and heroic soul is disguised in a sick or deformed body.

The Extent of This Evil

An investigation of 270 students in a North American university found 240 of them with feelings of frustration or deficiency, physical inability, a not very sympathetic presence, conflicting loves, little aptitude for study or social life, and remorse.

There are students with brilliant compositions in a written examination whom fear of the examiners will disturb and make awkward in an oral examination. Inexperienced orators and poets, who have prepared magnificent compositions, at the sight of an exacting audience will begin to tremble. They will grow pale, stutter, and even forget what they have learned or prepared. Too severe criticism had, after their first trials, cut their wings for life. There are well-trained men who after a failure in business or at one job think themselves unsuited for new ventures. And there are people who converse pleasantly and act courteously who one day are caught ill prepared. We see them grow mute, flush when they have to participate in a social event, and finally change into misanthropic solitaries. Typists, pianists, children, and young people who are extraordinarily gifted in private or within their family circle often seem nonentities in the presence of other people.

This timidity must not be confused with humility, for it sometimes arises from pride. It causes its victim no little suffering from blushing, trembling, palpitations, and stammering. These symptoms appear and disappear without apparent cause. They can even bring on lasting phobias or a mental inhibition. When they border on an emotional shock, they weaken or paralyze the muscles. Humility is not depressing. It is truth and raises one up toward God and confidence in Him.

You must war against so widespread an evil. Above all, do not cause such a feeling in children or youths by continually reminding them of and exaggerating their defects. They must, on the contrary, be encouraged and shown their possibilities for progress. Do not, even as a joke, give a child terror of ghosts, the dead, darkness, or animals. This will probably remain active in his subconscious even after he has grown up.

On the contrary, you must encourage and show them how to make progress. Manage things so that they do triumph in some matter; get them to be outstanding in something. Little by little get them to face up to difficulties and conquer them. Teach them to use their liberty well, to undertake tasks that are gradually more difficult, to make decisions and assume responsibilities for themselves. And when they fail or fear failure, help them to overcome even this by convincing them that they should not be discouraged but should profit from their failure (or fear of failure), learn how to get on their feet again, and so develop even greater strength.

Cure

If you find this timidity in yourself, calmly examine the thoughts and motives which cause it. Remove exaggerated deductions from your subconsciousness and have trust in yourself. Make an examination of your timidity in writing and show this to your director or mental adviser. You know that there is no reason for being a coward, that all men are equal, that you are superior to most in your own specialty, that there are many mediocre people, that geniuses know how to cover up their deficiencies and show their good qualities. Soak yourself in these ideas. Boil them down into suggestive formulas and frequently repeat them, especially when signs of timidity appear.

With such convictions and suggestions attack the emotional difficulties. Begin with the easier ones. Take courage at every victory, often repeating, "I am going to win out," "Each time I have more courage," and so forth. Never use negative formulas or conjure up the memory of phobias or symptoms which disturb you. If you say, for instance, "I am not going to blush," "I won't tremble," "I won't stammer," you will produce the very effect you wish to avoid.

Timid people usually remember their failures and easily forget their triumphs. To modify this negative memory, they should not think voluntarily about any past failure. On the contrary, they should note down their daily successes and those of the past. In moments of discouragement, they will profit from reading over these notes.

There is also a *supernatural* remedy to use. Let them stir up their faith in God who appreciates us, loves us, and can help us. Draw the conclusion from this: "Humble, yes; timid, no." For "I can do all things in Him who strengthens me." We should accept our limitations, then, for we are all clay as well as spirit. In Adam we have all fallen, but Christ has raised us up; He calls us, and we are in truth "adopted children of God."

Blushing and Embarrassment

A very common manifestation of a feeling of inferiority is the habit of blushing and the obvious embarrassment which accompanies it. For this reason, we should never make fun of those who blush easily. Suffering is always something sacred and should be respected even when it is subjective in origin. Sometimes it can have very deep roots in wounded self-love, something we did not—or do not—want to accept or admit. The aid of a specialist will then be very useful in discovering and overcoming such a deep-rooted wish. In ordinary cases we should not give importance to so natural and common a phenomenon. For it only indicates modesty and virtue (bad people do not blush). Go ahead *as if* this did not matter to you and take a greater part in the conversation. Pay more attention to what is being said or done. Let this attention fill the field of your consciousness. With no attention given them, the illusions suggested by timidity and caused by blushing will disappear.

One young teacher who blushed and sweated before his students was greatly impressed and cured by the following reasoning process. "If in spite of feeling myself beginning to blush, I go on firmly and energetically without worrying about it, then I am not inferior to others, but greater and stronger than all of them. For almost anyone else would act like a coward in these circumstances."

The means of conquering fear or timidity which have been explained above, especially those which give support to one's personality, are also advisable as a cure for unreasonable blushing. In particular one might try to reproduce in his mind the circumstances in which he blushed without cause. Let him imagine these vividly and think of himself as serene, then speak about them, using a tone of voice of absolute security.

One day Father Laburu[18] was asked to interview a young man, twenty-five years old, who blushed in the presence of anyone whomsoever. Father Laburu discovered that this had been going on since the young man was eleven years old. One day he had done something wrong on the way to school. The teacher called upon him to recite, and at once he blushed. Asked why he blushed so violently, he lied. This bothered him so much that on the following day he blushed again

---

[18] *Psicología Médica*, by Father J. A. de Laburu, S.J., Montevideo: Mosca Hermanos, 1945 (lectures delivered in the University of Buenos Aires).

while reciting. Then it started to happen while speaking to his father and later with other persons, too. Father Laburu discovered the cause for him and had him reproduce in his imagination the original circumstances which made such a strong impression on him. He had him recite after him, and with the same controlled tone of voice, "I am in front of my father and feel calm, completely secure, and happy." As soon as he succeeded in pronouncing these words with a tone of security, he felt transformed.

For a bodily treatment I recommend for you any tonic or strengthener of the nervous system, breathing exercises, sports, or any moderate physical exercise. Practice sureness of gaze, not that you should seem to be staring or boldly provocative or trying to pierce behind a companion's eyes. But practice a gaze which looks easily and dignifiedly at a point between another person's eyes. If you have photophobia (that is, if light bothers you) keep your back to the source of the light or use tinted glasses.

Superiors or directors who treat with timid people will do well not to look at their eyes or forehead or even sit directly in front of them, but toward the side. Thus, the timid will be less bashful and more confident. Nor should they be required before special training to perform acts of self-conquest in which a great objective difficulty comes more from timidity or phobias than pride or a lack of mortification.

Orators who experience their breath growing shorter or being choked off just before stepping up onto the speaking platform should breathe deeply for five or ten seconds, emptying their lungs of used air. At the subsequent automatic filling of their lungs with pure air they will begin to speak with a sure voice and will conquer their timidity.

The Supernatural Remedy

For those who have faith the great remedy is a concrete and heroic confidence in God who can and will aid us. For He commands us "not to fear," not even "those who can kill the body." Their remedy is also confident and persevering prayer which obtains whatever it asks for. "The more you ask for when you pray, believe that you will receive it and it shall be given to you." Here as elsewhere we must avoid timidity. We must not make the future present, for where the future is made present it is disfigured. The only time that exists is now. The past did exist, but does no longer; the future may exist, but does not yet. The only two important times, as Catholics acknowledge in the Hail Mary, are "now and at the hour of our death."

Values to Think About

"*Per angusta ad augusta*," said the ancient Romans. In other words, the road to grandeur leads through difficulties.

"*Patientia opus perfectum habet*" (James 1:4). In other words, patience is the secret of perfection. Patience will every day bring me some improvement and some useful experience.

A bent blade of grass is not dead but can raise itself up anew.

There is no night so dark but that some lamp is shining.

Whatever does not conquer me makes me stronger. Only a dead fish drifts downstream without being able to swim against the current.

Each day we can learn to see better the face of suffering and convert it into joy. Each day I can better see the good side of things and learn how to use them better for a good purpose.

No failure should cause me to lose a joyful and optimistic hope for the eventual success of our undertakings.

If I learn how to profit from the lesson, even defeat will be transformed into strength.

Just as knowing how to fall correctly is necessary for certain sports, so for victory in life we must know how to win even when we are beaten. We must learn how to fall without discouragement, to lose without irritation, to fail without despair, to suffer without sadness.

I can do all things in Him who strengthens me.

If God be with us, who shall stand against us? If the Almighty is with me, whom shall I fear?

OUTLINE DIAGRAM

How to Control Feelings

In general

A chaotic force: direct it

Do not be governed by likes or dislikes, but by reason

Govern them
- by lessening their exaggerations
- making no change merely on their account
- thinking about the opposite
- working against the feeling

Their release
- Useful — in affective conflicts, noble affections
- Useless — impulsive confidences
- Harmful — from passion

In parrticular

Dominate anger
- Controlling thoughts
- Thinking about something else, the opposite
- Working "as if . . ."

Feeling of inferiority

Causes
- Failures, defects, criticisms
- Fear of "what they will say"

Effects
- Suffering, apprehensive fear, embarrassment (blushing), paralysis, irritation

Remedies

Preventive
- Not to exaggerate faults
- Not to instill vain fears

Curative
- Examine the root cause and its path
- Conviction and suggestion of courage
- Attack difficulties by degrees

Supernatural remedies
- Confidence
- Prayer

13

Sadness

The emotion of sadness is due to the idea of *failure* in an action or enterprise, the idea of *frustration* of some desire or hope, or frustration in life itself, the idea of *lack* or *loss* of a good, or the idea of a *present evil* which we synthesize in the word "suffering." It will be the more acute and penetrating as the loss is greater or seems greater, and all the more paralyzing as the remedy seems far away. It will be a negative sadness or despair if the three concepts of *loss*, *total* loss, and *irreparable* loss are joined together. Hence no sadness can be greater than that which accompanies the thought of hell, where the loss is evidently infinite and without remedy for all eternity.

There are specific harms resulting from sadness in addition to the usual effects of all depressive emotions, e.g., fatigue, hypertension, arthritis, asthma, and digestive and circulatory disturbances. In two words, sadness "slows down and paralyzes." Sadness slows down all one's vitality, efficiency, health, nutritional processes, etc., and sometimes paralyzes them. If there is exaggeration in the idea of loss, this can become obsessing and prevent us from attending to other things, especially when it is also joined to an emotion of fear or disgust.

These effects may also extend to one's spiritual and social life. To serve God with sadness while He is heaping benefits upon us is to dishonor and displease Him. Boredom and tepidity will soon follow. A life of virtue will seem intolerable, and an illusory and harmful compensation may be sought for in luxury. Our neighbor, too, is annoyed by our sad eyes, for these emit rays of sadness and tell him that he does not please us.

Predisposing Causes

The *organic* cause of this emotion or, better, the temperamental predisposition to hold on to sad thoughts and feelings can have its origin in general illness or a specific infirmity, especially in one connected with the stomach or liver. It may also come from prolonged fatigue, or the chronic tiredness of elderly people.

The predisposing *psychical* causes are manifold.

1. *Perfectionism.* When we build up for ourselves a utopian ideal which goes beyond our own capacity or expects too much from others, we become "perfectionists." We may make our happiness depend upon *excessive* demands for personal attentions, comforts, entertainment, success, and so forth. Then the idea of frustration in not having these demands satisfied will always be plaguing us. We should remedy this by accepting our limitations and not aiming at or hoping for so very much satisfaction, so many attentions from others, or so many personal triumphs for ourselves. In brief, we should not set the price of happiness so high.

2. *Negativism.* This is often the result of a childhood experience in which our elders kept harping on our defects and

the defects of others. As children, then, we did not learn how to discover the good in ourselves or others. Or perhaps we ourselves are responsible for developing a negative and pessimistic attitude because of a habit of recalling to mind our difficulties and personal defects, forgetting the victories and joys of life. In such cases, instead of developing a positive and optimistic tendency, the master-idea of our life becomes the idea of loss or failure.

The pessimist will say about a rose: "Too bad it has thorns." An optimist, on the other hand, will see the thorns and say, "It's wonderful that thorns can protect so beautiful a flower." The pessimist is sad at thinking that one day is surrounded by two nights; the optimist is joyful at expecting two days with one night. The former sees that a bottle is half empty; to the latter it is still half full.

3. *Hysterical egoism.* This type wants to seem to be a "victim" so that others will take pity on him. He will talk about and exaggerate his ills and sadness as a "bid" to attract attention.

4. *A predisposition to sadness.* Hunger for appreciation is never sated. Sometimes in childhood we experience a kind of anxiety for affection and, when we do not get it, we feel that our rights have been violated. Sometimes in later life we feel that we have been frustrated or unsuccessful in love, and this vacuum of affection can continue for the rest of one's life and easily lead to a chronic state of sadness. One example: a missionary whom I knew in the Far East often used to experience a feeling of frustration despite his sacrifices and generosity with God and souls. He became so sad that he began to doubt whether he had a true vocation. I asked him one question: "Were you treated affectionately as

a child?" He lowered his eyes and answered, "I never knew my mother, and my father never showed us any affection." Then I hinted that this affective vacuum could explain his present state and in no way indicated a lack of vocation. At this he felt greatly relieved. His spirits rose and he set out to compensate for that defect by deliberately taking means to feel the infinite love of God for him and making a return of his own love to God. He also expressed this in work for the service of his neighbor—with whom Christ wished to identify Himself.

The hunger for affection may come from an opposite source if, for instance, as children, we were treated with so much indulgence that this became a kind of second nature to us. Later when this strain of constant affection and indulgence slackened off, as it normally does, we would tend to think we were missing something essential.

5. But the greatest cause of sadness is the *horror of suffering,* a refusal of physical or moral pain, seeing nothing but evil in it, not attending to the good it brings with it, looking upon the slightest difficulty as a tragedy and, with all this, an excessive anticipation of future sufferings, imminent failure, or a painful death.

Instead, we should recall that events never turn out so badly as we fear or so well as we dream they will. There are many mistakes in our calculations about the future. At the end of our lives, we shall discover that we suffered by anticipation many ills which never came our way at all. "Sufficient for the day is the evil thereof," said Our Lord Jesus Christ. There is no need to outdo Divine Providence. We know that God will not permit greater sufferings than we are able to bear, nor more sufferings than will be useful to us. We also know that He Himself will help us overcome them.

As for the thought of a painful death which predisposes so many people to sadness, recall what doctors and actual experience teach us. Death will come either from a paralysis of the brain, and then there is no suffering because sensation is annihilated, or from a paralysis of the heart or lungs, and then there follows a state of stupefaction from the accumulation of carbonic acid. In such a state there is no real physical pain even though the body exhibits reflex actions and contortions. As for moral suffering, the Divine Goodness will take this away from those who serve God with good will.

The immediate cause of the emotion of sadness will always be, as we have indicated above, a thought or idea of failure, frustration, lack, loss, or present evil. Such a thought may exist clearly in our mind or confusedly in our subconscious.

Remedies

First Remedy

The first remedy is to take the ideas which cause sadness in us and make them concrete, analyze them, correct, and control them. These may be ideas of (a) failure or mistake, (b) inability or sickness, (c) death of a loved one, (d) sorrow or trouble in general.

a. *Failure* in a career or business enterprise, or even being called upon to speak in public when unprepared, produces sadness when we think, "I have wasted my time, looked like a fool, or lost my head." In such instances happiness depends upon whether we are able to oppose this thought with a balancing truth such as, "I lost a dollar, but gained a million." This will always be a consoling truth if we act with a good intention. Whenever we are friends of God through grace and act with good will, our Heavenly Father writes for us a heavenly check for eternal glory and satisfaction. We have then gained a million, though we may have lost certain creatures, things of little value, insignificant grains of sand compared with the Infinite. Can such a situation be a sad one?

A mistake can be purely subjective when, for instance, we expect more than what is reasonable. But there is a means of ensuring joy. When we do favors for others, we should not look for human gratitude. For a human return is very often lacking, especially as regards work done for the common good. Let us act, instead, in order to please God who receives as done for Him what we do for our neighbor and who promises to pay us back with an "eternal kingdom."

b. *Inability and sickness* sadden us with the idea that we are burdensome to others, do not produce anything, and merely suffer. The aged and infirm feel more strongly about this to the extent that their youth was active. If only they could understand that, for eternal results, patience and prayer are more effective than all our merely human initiative and activity.

I explained this to some old people in a nursing home and asked them to be missionaries through patience. Afterward the nursing sisters could not get over their astonishment at seeing the vitality which this thought brought them. The same thing happened with a twelve-year-old boy who had been in the hospital for three months. I asked him if he would like to be a missionary and save souls.

"But, Father, I can't even sit up in bed. I can hardly move."

"Exactly. If you offer your sufferings for souls, you can save them better than I. You see, Jesus Christ preached and performed many miracles, but only a few people were converted. When He suffered and died, though, He redeemed the whole world."

Hearing this, the youngster began to cry.

"Why are you crying?"

"Because I have lost a year of suffering. Why didn't someone tell me this a year ago?"

From then on, he cried no more. Instead, the more he suffered, the happier he became. For he was helping to save more souls.

c. *Death itself* cannot take joy away from a Christian family. If the death of a loved one makes us sad, this is usually because we look at him and imagine, like the pagans, that at death he has lost everything. Or because we look at ourselves and think that "we have lost him." This phrase is so often used erroneously. But if we activate our faith and convince ourselves of the happiness of those who die in the Lord, and the help which, with Him, they can bring us, then we can feel consolation and joy.

d. *A present difficulty or "trouble"* will not make us sad if, instead of looking at its unpleasant side, we see it in the light of faith. Suffering should be an imitation of God who took suffering upon Himself in this life. Our pain is a completion of what is lacking, as St. Paul says, in the sufferings of Christ. It makes the application of the merits of His Passion more effective. More souls can be saved as a result of our sufferings if they are united with those of Christ.

Trouble is a check drawn upon the bank of heaven. If we understood God's own language, we would read in it this idea: "Infinite Justice and Goodness promise to pay back in heaven a superhuman and endless glory and satisfaction to the Christian who, while in the state of grace, willingly accepts a light and passing suffering." The divine signature is put on this check only when we accept the suffering. Day by day to pile up such checks for eternity is a source of happiness; and it is a great good fortune to suffer only lightly and for an instant as the price of gaining infinite joy forever.

We must know how to value suffering and how to handle the thorns of life. If we tread on them, they torment us; in our conscience they kill us; in our heart they stir up life. Under our feet they prevent our walking; in our conscience they block true life; in our heart they let us fly. This power they have from the Heart of Christ.

Second Remedy

The second remedy is to *foment thoughts of joy.* We should always have optimistic thoughts, happy memories, and a clear acknowledgment of God's benefits in that treasure house of creation, human nature. We should also increase our knowledge and cheerfully think about the inexhaustible treasures offered us in the world of color, form, and sound. Artists usually catch a vision of all this and know how to appreciate it.

Our eyes are marvelously perfect cameras. Automatically they focus upon, capture, and project into our brain living scenes in full color and three dimensions. Our sense of hearing is like a marvelous internal musical instrument which faithfully reproduces thousands of different notes and melodies. Our hands, arms, and legs are like cranes which can execute an infinite variety of complicated movements. In brief, our whole organism is a marvelous treasure created for us by God. This is especially true of our memory, a library which classifies, in order, thousands of useful experiences; our understanding which continually discovers more and more of reality and will be able to understand Infinite Reality; and our will by which we are capable of union with Uncreated Goodness.

Recognize, too, the many goods we have in the family, State, and Church, and all the supernatural means we have of getting to Heaven. This is a happy thought because of the certitude we have from faith and reason that God exists and is Our Father, that He is with us, watches over us, and governs all our circumstances for our benefit. This is, moreover, a calming and peaceful thought, for hope in the divine promises gives us a foretaste of Heaven. There is, in addition, a thrill of joy and satisfaction in the thought that we are the objects of God's love and can ourselves sincerely love Him.

Third Remedy

The third remedy is to *change* negative attitudes and habits, which are the cause of sadness and depression, for those which are positive and joyful. We should get used to extracting from ordinary day-to-day life whatever can increase our joy, rest, and legitimate satisfaction, and whatever can fill us with optimism. We should avoid the thoughts which bring disillusionment, envy, or discouragement. To this end we should act as follows.

a. *Lead a simpler life,* with fewer demands for food, rest, entertainment, travel, and so on. Learn how to find satisfaction in a modest quantity of all these things. There you have the secret of happiness and equanimity. Many millionaires are pressured by worries, ulcers, and insomnia. They yearn longingly for the days of their youth. They may have worked very hard when they were young, but at that time an ordinary meal gave them full satisfaction, a hard bed perfect repose, and a simple game in the open fields complete diversion.

b. *Find enjoyment in your work.* If you do not, a negative emotion of impatience or disgust will constantly be nagging at you. We should find pleasure in a job well done, useful for others, and of value to ourselves in eternity. Then there will be no time to be bored. An idle life that needs continual and costly entertainment may satisfy a child, but no adult can find completion in it. For an adult needs to be convinced that he is using his time to some avail.

c. Make your life one of *continual satisfaction and positive feelings.* Obviously there will be interruptions in this satisfaction when we run into evident negligence, incompetence, or bad will. But even these will have excusing or attenuating causes. And if we look at what patience can produce for us in Heaven, these occasions may even bring us joy. Let us not bemoan the inevitable, bad weather, etc. Neither should we attempt what is impossible. On the contrary, look for and find in your existential situations motives of joy and satisfaction: the blue of the skies, colors of the field, the habits of birds and insects, the variety and beauty of flowers, plants, and sounds. In the roof which protects us, the hearts which love us, society that helps us, God Himself is caring for us and preparing us with an Infinite Love for a happiness to come which is more than human. So look for the good in all things and find pleasure in cooperating with it. Always have a pleasant and kind word to say that will bring joy to others, cheer to yourself, and peace all round. A "thank you" to the porter, elevator operator, or taxi driver costs nothing, but can sweeten an embittered life.

One man in Havana came to me to seek a remedy for his "great unhappiness." He had a wife with a defect which made her hard to live with. This defect was a temperamental one, and she was hardly responsible for it at all. I asked him to come back again in two days and, in the meanwhile, to think over and write down his wife's good qualities. He came back to thank me, already cured. He understood that he had a precious diamond with thirty-three brilliant sides to it and only one small scratch on its surface.

Fourth Remedy

The fourth remedy is the expression of joy, a *smile,* even when our negative thoughts and attitudes have lasted so long that they have engraved in us a feeling or tendency to sadness. We must try to implant the contrary feeling even in the subconscious. Do that by joyful thoughts and conversation and, most of all, by that expression of satisfaction, a smile. This satisfaction and joy should be expressed with one's whole being, an open laugh, smiling eyes, cheerful words, a happy song, a contented tone of voice, relaxed breathing. We should smile *joyfully* when things go well, and *bravely* in time of suffering.

a. Smile *when things go well* and everything is on your side, when you can seize upon the great good that there is in the world, the good you possess yourself and that others have, and all the good that God wishes to give you. This external expression of satisfaction helps to tone up the whole organism, facilitates the process of nutrition, and relaxes tension. With joy our understanding is sharper, our thinking clearer, our imagination more vivid, our soul more serene, and our will stronger. A pleasant smile attracts one's neighbor, glorifies God, makes virtue easy and sacrifice sweet.

b. You should also smile *bravely in sorrow*. Whenever you suffer, deliberately have more joy, like the organist who overcomes outside noise by playing the organ with vigor. Smile to convince yourself that the little misfortunes and indispositions that would tend to make a strong impression on you are really insignificant. By smiling accelerate a positive reaction against the very first movements of impatience or disgust. Smile at once to block the very first depressing tendency or its growth. Smile and sing to get the strength to act "as if" you were content. There is no way to prevent you from being happy at all times because the one thing necessary, doing God's will, is always near at hand.

In Brazil I was asked to visit a lady who had spent six months without going out of her house, always weeping and wailing over the death of her son. Her sleep and appetite were gone. She seemed to be on the brink of moral and physical breakdown, despite the medications prescribed by her doctor. As soon as I arrived, she cried out, "I am so unhappy. Six months ago, I lost my son." Because she was a Christian and because her son had died as a good Christian, I said to her, "Lady, take that back! Six months ago you gained your son." And I explained this to her graphically to make an impression on her imagination. "You were going along in one ship across the stormy sea of life, and your son in another. All of a sudden, a friendly wind and a friendly hand brought your son to the safe harbor of salvation while you go on, tossed about by the storms of life. Isn't it true that six months ago you gained your son?" She accepted the explanation, but with her intellect only. To complete her cure, feelings had to enter. So I then said, "Say after me, and in the same tone of voice as I, this sentence: I am happy, for six months ago I gained my son." It cost her a great deal to repeat that sentence and to produce the tone of satisfaction with which I pronounced it. But when she understood my explanation, that this very tone of voice would produce in her the feeling of joy that she needed, she repeated it so earnestly that she was immediately transformed.

Existential Sadness and Anxiety

Sometimes sadness and fear can have roots that are very deep and far reaching. A vague idea of loss or danger can seem to be part of one's very being and dominate everything earthly and passing. This often happens in people without sufficient faith or religious practice. Their innate tendency toward God and toward true and endless happiness seems to have been repressed and frustrated. This can cause painful feelings and even bring them to a neurotic state. According to Dr. Viktor Frankl, one-third of the neuroses in Europe have this as their cause. The remedy consists in allowing our transcendental tendencies to extend themselves outward by means of a more perfectly realized knowledge of a personal God, who is our Father, governing the universe for our good and by a more perfect realization of the end for which we have been placed in this world—that is, to love and serve this Heavenly Father and afterward enjoy His company forever in heaven.

We ought to put aside at once, then, every sad thought or memory and think habitually about the treasures we do possess, natural or supernatural, present or future. Keep the following sayings in mind, after meditating upon them, and they will help you accomplish this.

All goes well, for everywhere God stands as a loving Father behind everything and guiding every event beforehand.

I cannot be sad, granted that the Infinite God loves me and wants me to be happy.

Suffering is a check drawn upon heaven which brings joy to the noblest part of my being.

We are worth what we can redeem; the size of our cross is the measure of our greatness.

My life will be very useful; by prayer and suffering I can save many souls.

Be happy because at every moment you can be as pleasing to God as possible by doing what He wants and wanting what He does.

My happiness is immense, for a God of love dwells in my soul through grace.

The best remedy for sadness is to learn how to be happy. This is explained in the following chapter where we gather together in one place those ideas that are scattered through the whole book.

14

How to Be Happy

Happiness is not found but made. It does not depend on what you do not have, but on the use you make of what you do have. It is not something far from yourself but the most intimate part of your being. It is the consciousness of a good, and the greater and more lasting this is, the greater will be your happiness.

You need not travel many lands to find happiness, nor burden yourself with back-breaking labors to win it. It is enough to follow your own road, the road of duty. If you can control your thoughts, you will be able to find the flower of joy even among the thorns of suffering.

We all strive for happiness. God wants us to be happy. He repeats it a thousand times in the Scripture and liturgy. "My peace I leave with you." "Your joy no one will take from you." "Rejoice always in the Lord." "Alleluia." Joy is possible, then, in all circumstances of life.

However, there are many who do not find it because they go looking for it where it is not to be found, in vice or illicit pleasure. And so, upon returning within themselves, they find their heart empty and feel tedium, disgust, and sadness. They try to forget by means of amusements, movies, parties, novels, and so on. But they do not get rid of the cause of their unhappiness, nor do they give their heart the satisfaction of duty done. They are satisfied with merely hiding their lack of happiness.

"Joy," says Aristotle, "is the accompaniment of a perfect act." Now an act against conscience or duty is essentially vitiated or imperfect. It can then produce, even after some momentary delight, only a deep and lasting sadness. But even those who strive for joy where it may be found sometimes find only suffering, and because of this they drown themselves in a sea of sadness. Yet suffering should not be an obstacle to your joy. The bee draws honey from flowers, and the soul can draw honey from thorns. But this process is patented—in Christianity.

Objective Suffering

Suffering can be an objective thing; for example, the sickness, poverty, or failures which God positively wants you to suffer. It can also be mostly subjective, the effects which the first type produces in you and which you do not control. These effects are sadness, worry, and fear which God only permits. Here what He positively wants is your reaction to them, your control of them.

Be happy, then, "negatively" by overcoming objective suffering. Convert it into joy. How? By shifting your gaze from the unpleasant aspect, from the ugly face of suffering, and concentrating on the bright side. Mentally you have this power, acquired by the re-education of concentration. (See Part 1 of this book.)

Suffering actually has two sides to it, a pleasant and an unpleasant side. The unpleasant side contradicts your tendencies, sensuality, natural inclinations, pride, self-will. Do not fix your attention on this unpleasant side. Suffering has a pleasant side also. In the natural order suffering can be pleasant because it brings an increase of experience, strength, counsel, and patience. But this natural side alone is but small consolation. Hence the difficulty in comforting atheists, but how easy to comfort Christians! Considered in the supernatural order, suffering is exceedingly attractive. It is the role which, while on earth, God chose for Himself. It is the livery of Jesus Christ. It is a check which God offers us. If we accept it, God signs it and our happiness in Heaven will be proportionate to its value. It is the secret treasure of the Cross, made known to and through the saints. And it is the fruit of devotion to the Heart of Jesus. Supernaturally, then, we are able to increase this inclination to suffering and find our joy in it. It is integral to Christianity, the apex of virtue, the grandeur of the saints whose joy no human event could disturb.

St. Paul said, "I am filled with joy because of my tribulations." St. Peter recommended, "Be filled with joy in your sufferings." The Apostles "left the tribunal joyfully because they had been judged worthy to suffer insults and sorrow for Jesus Christ."

St. Ignatius Loyola attained complete dominion over his feelings. The doctor forbade him to think about sad things. He examined himself. The saddest of all would be the total destruction of the Society of Jesus. Yet he decided that fifteen minutes of prayer would be enough to reconcile himself even to this.

St. Francis Xavier had such consolation in the Molucca Islands where he suffered so much that he exclaimed, "It is enough, Lord. I shall die of joy."

St. Theresa used to repeat, "Either to suffer or to die." And St. Mary Magdalene de Pazzi used to say, "Not to die, but to suffer!"

On the missions, as a matter of fact, the missionary's greatest consolation after a day of suffering is to repeat before the Tabernacle, "For you, O Lord!"

It is within your power, then, to change objective suffering into joy instead of sorrow.

Subjective Sorrow

In the face of present or imminent disgrace any normal person first feels a sense of dejection and worry. But by considering its attractive aspect he soon controls these feelings and they do not last very long. However, in sick or nervous people such feelings keep coming back and become obsessions. They produce persistent sadness, phobias, or scruples which destroy all peace and joy. These are crosses which God permits, but which He wants you to control. You must then fight and get control of them.

Control of Subjective Sorrow

1. In addition to the explanations in chapter 10, in case of sorrow or internal conflict, *express your feelings externally* in consultation. Make them known as soon as possible to your director or confessor. Tell him of moral acts which burden your conscience, harrowing doubts or indecisions, fears which get control of you. This manifestation with its psychological and supernatural solution will resolve your internal conflict and sorrow.

2. *Live in the present.* The present is a fount of joy. There are delights which crave to be yours. They are external creation

(aesthetic pleasure) and moral beauty. So give them entrance by attending to the present. You should not think about the sorry past which has already slipped from your hands. Leave it to the mercy of God. And think not on the agony of an uncertain future. Leave this to His providence. The present is a pleasant path which runs between two chasms, the past and the future. Whoever by sadness or scruples falls into the past, or slips by worry into the future, ceases advancing toward his happiness.

3. *Live a conscious life.* "*Age quod agis*" ("Do what you're doing"). If you work on a conscious level, fear, worry, and sadness will find no place to torment you. Thus you will lessen and even suppress the influence of a sad and uncontrolled subconscious. "We stand in need of happy people," writes Marden, "who look away from the sinful, bitter, and perverse world and turn toward God's world to admire its beauty and perfection."

4. *Practice voluntary concentration on other matters.* These concentrations may be indifferent in relation to those which the unconscious tries to impose on you. If sadness or worry is besieging you, concentrate on some study or occupation that pleases you. Even better, concentrate on something directly opposed. For instance, against fear or disturbance concentrate on living images of peace, control and energy. In this war you must take the offensive in order to rout the enemy even from his lair in the unconscious.

Cultivate the habit of joy. Your mental makeup is a labyrinthine wood. Your thoughts and acts are men who are tracing a path through it. Where one has passed, the easier it is for the next. So then, if you would win the heights of joy, you must send joyful thoughts through to open up the trail. Repeat them and reinforce them with acts of satisfaction and optimism until you have enlarged the trail and made it firm through habit. Then, almost without noticing it, you will find you are always happy.

5. *Practice will acts.* Will the contrary feeling; that is, be animated, tranquil, kind, happy. Talk and work *as if* you did not feel the opposite feeling (antipathy, worry, fear) or *as if* you were animated, happy, and so forth.

6. *Use suggestion.* At night before falling beneath the dominion of the unconscious and in the morning when leaving its control, think with feeling about images of peace, control, and joy. Repeat to yourself: "Everything I do can be a step taken nearer to God," "Every day I am increasing in sanctifying grace," "Every day I am happier."

7. *Moderate your desires and aspirations.* Keep them within reasonable limits. Seek not for body or soul or anything else a greater security, health, or prosperity than God wishes it to have in this world. Thus scruples or worry will lessen or disappear.

8. *Overcome negative and depressive feelings.* Do this by introducing other feelings which are positive, sublime, and ennobling, such as love of an ideal, of God, souls, or Heaven. Overcome petty, low, and disordered self-love with true love of yourself and your spiritual and eternal good. Before this sublime reality all fears, sadness, and phobias fall to earth.

Happiness in this life is not divorced from sacrifice. Our satisfaction increases in the measure that we make those who surround us happy, that we seek the greater glory of God, and in proportion to our sacrifices toward this end.

Positive Happiness

You can have a happiness and joy which is not external and vain but interior, true, and well founded, one which fills your heart with satisfaction. This happiness has four aspects and comes to us through as many channels:

- *Aesthetic pleasure* by which we receive within us the beauty of the external world through conscious sensations, when we contemplate the beauties of nature or of the arts, and especially when we do this in the light and warmth of an ideal. (See chapters 3, 7, and 15.)
- *Intellectual pleasure* when by intellectual concentration we possess the truth with certitude, and perfect it or complete it by analysis and synthesis. (See chapter 3.)
- *Volitional satisfaction* in the power of producing, and in doing, what we value. This type of happiness is the result of exercising a firm and constant will (chapters 3 and 8).
- *Emotional or affective satisfaction* at feeling one's own kindness irradiating others, and the kindness of others being diffused in oneself through the elevation and equanimity of our feelings (chapters 5, 10, 14).

Your human capital is twofold: your faculties and the time for making them produce. You can have no true satisfaction if you see your capital diminishing each day yet bringing you no return. Nor can you have any satisfaction if you feel your time passing in useless amusements or occupations. You ought not to feel that each passing moment is lost or less profitable. You should feel that it is a source of your own and your neighbor's well-being, and a fruitful seed of an immortal and happy life in Heaven.

To bring about this satisfaction and sense of fulfillment, the "life" element should also be present in a vigorous functioning of your intellect and will. Then you will find in your mental concept of happiness the characteristics of unity and totality.

The scholar who makes a discovery has great intellectual pleasure. The mother who is always loving and showing her love for her child is very happy even in the midst of work and sufferings. If that pleasure of the scholar were not disturbed by other ideas and distractions and were prolonged by new and more brilliant findings, and if that of the mother had as its object not a mortal child with all its imperfections but one which would never be separated from her and had all possible good qualities, then we would have true, complete mental happiness. Before it, all merely bodily happiness would grow pale, fade, and pass away. You could sum it up in these words: *fullness and unity of your mind and feelings.*

Now let us see how this happiness, though limited in this world, yet unlimited, secure, and eternal in the next, is in a real and true sense near at hand. With re-education of control presupposed, apply your understanding to knowing not some small part of the truth but all the truth, infinite truth, truth in itself, God. Each day you can discover new horizons without ever exhausting this infinite fountain of truth and beauty. This is the joy of spiritual persons at receiving in prayer those supernatural lights which we call divine consolations. These eclipse all worldly happiness and cannot even be imagined by those who have not experienced them.

Dedicate your will and feelings to loving the infinitely lovable good, God. Strive to realize that He is not far off from you, but close by in all created things. In these He is at your service and gives you joy. Try to possess Him in the Eucharist, human in body as you yourself. And enjoy a holy intimacy with Him, present as He is within you through sanctifying grace.

This is the type of joy in union with God that made a St. Francis of Assisi complain of the sun that it rose too early and forced him to leave the delights of a night with God. Happiness impelled St. Ignatius, when he saw a flower, to say with tears of consolation, "Be silent, be quiet for I understand you." He would remain in ecstatic contemplation of the Divine Beauty of which the flower was but a pale reflection.

Speaking before a Youth Congress of Catholic Action, one of the leaders said, "At first in prayer I used to look toward Heaven, but ever since I realized that God was within me, I look toward myself and feel great joy." Tears came to his eyes and were joined to those of his listeners. He was happy at loving and feeling God within himself. That is why the great mystics who felt the presence of God in this world speak so many marvels about this little-known happiness.

St. John of the Cross insists that the devil admitted to him that if he had a body and if, in order to see God, he would have to climb a pole studded with thorns and needles, he would not hesitate to do this for ten thousand years in exchange for enjoying the sight of God for a single minute.

Some Thoughts on Changing Sorrow into Joy

Passing over the threshing floor, the southwest wind raises eddies of dust. But, sweeping through flower gardens, it raises a cloud of perfumes. So does the wind of suffering act differently in different souls.

The Divine Heart of infinite happiness is "bound with thorns."
If you feel the touch of thorns in your heart, it is a sign that
God is reaching out His heart to you, a sign of the embrace
of Infinite Happiness. But happiness will enter into you only
through your wounds. God left a trail of blood at His pas-
sage through the world; no longer can there be doubt about
which is the path to glory, the road to permanent happiness.

Acceptance of sorrow is a contract for work made with
God. You agree to construct some great thing with Him.
You are the workman who does not see the plans. God is the
architect with sublime and magnificent designs.

Nothing great is accomplished without suffering and humiliation, says Newman, and everything is possible by using
these means. We must be friendly with suffering. It is a selfless
and faithful friend which reminds us of true goods. Souls
are instructed by word of mouth but are saved by sacrifice.

Some Thoughts on Happiness and Joy

Happiness is a noble, peaceful, and recollected lady who
dwells in the hidden fortress of the soul. She knows and tastes
its treasures. Frequently she shows herself at the windows of
the face and wreathes it with a smile. She clothes the face
thus with the brilliance of rational being. This is something
about which neither animals nor the most beautiful flowers
can boast.

When the polished, peaceful mirror of consciousness
reflects a ray of the sun, some good possessed or soon to
come, its spontaneous reflection is joy, a smile. If the sun of
Infinite Good shines directly upon it, it will reflect happiness.

Life should be a perpetual joy, the joy of living for God,
of serving Him in one's neighbor, of saving souls, the austere

joy found in suffering. There is the joy of living in a present of infinite value, joy for a past entrusted to the Divine Mercy, joy for a future assured by His Paternal Providence. Have joy in work, and if this is beyond your powers, then have joy in prayer. If even this seems impossible for you, then have joy at least in suffering in Christ and for the sake of Heaven.

The apostle who takes doctrine and example and, together with these, sows smiles, and then waters these with prayers and sacrifices, will win many souls. "Joy," says St. Paul of the Cross, "is the sun of souls. It enlightens those who possess it and enlivens as many as receive its rays."

The exercise of Christian charity is the best way to make yourself joyful. And this is your most effective contribution to the happiness of others. Smiling eyes scatter more rays of joy than precious diamonds. Through joy you will better perform your duties. And your burdens will be lighter. It will be your consolation in solitude and your best introduction to society. You will be the more sought after, the more trusted, and better appreciated.

The vicious, degenerate, or low person may come on the stage of life as a loud and vulgar jester. But he is almost never sincerely happy. Almost never can he wholly forget what weighs upon his conscience. Evil is a cold hand which freezes smiles. But a frank and hearty smile is almost always an indication of a noble and pure heart. The virtue that smiles is the more beautiful and often the most heroic.

OUTLINE DIAGRAM

How to Be Happy

God wants you to be happy — Not in vice, nor only in amusements but in duty, and within you.

Negatively

Objective suffering (accept the misfortunes, etc. that God wants you to)

- Avoid pessimism — Contrary to desires, feelings, instincts
- Cultivate optimism
  - Natural — Gives experience, strength, counsel
  - Supernatural
    - Cross of Christ
    - His role on earth
    - A check drawn on Heaven
    - The great Architect
    - Example of the saints

Subjective sorrow (which depends on you)
- By expression, confidence, Confession
- Live in the present (aesthetic pleasure)
- Conscious life
- Concentration on joyful things
- Contrary actions and will acts
- Suggestion of peace and joy
- Moderated desires
- Deep implanting of sublime feelings

Positively

Intellectual
- A scholar's pleasure at attaining some truth
- Unlimited joy with all truth

Affective
- A mother's happiness in loving her child
- Highest happiness in loving and possessing all Goodness

Examples and sayings

15

Choice of a Vision for One's Life

A great life is the great dream of youth realized in mature age.

—Alfred de Vigny

All the advice of this book can be summarized into the choosing of an ideal vision for one's life. This is a shortcut to attain what we propose in the second part of the book. It is medicine, strength, joy, activity, and rest. It has produced geniuses, heroes, and saints.

There is a general or abstract ideal (learning, for example, or art, skill, service, sanctity, patriotism) which can be the goal of your actions. And this goal you can strip in your own mind of all possible defects and adorn with all good qualities. This becomes your particular ideal. The ideal chosen by you becomes the object of a tendency or inclination. It is a detailed picture of your forceful and permanent desire of the more general goal.

The Nature of an Ideal
The Intellectual Element

There is especially required, as the very word "ideal" indicates, a great idea (the general ideal). This is a concrete and constant idea, a goal, a purpose, a good that is precisely, clearly, and constantly foreseen. It is a fixed idea, a permanent attention, with all the power of concentration and action which this implies: "Fear the man of a single idea," says an old proverb.

The Feeling Element
Your ideal results in a fixed and instinctive tendency, at the same time sensible and spiritual. You are in a state of forceful impulse toward that good which constantly presents itself as fulfilling the aspirations of your being. It tends to attract related inclinations to itself and its own direction, and to repel opposed ones.

The Will or Executive Element
That permanent attention and feeling influences your will. As a result your will acquires a new force and constancy. And your ideal is then translated into repeated acts. It is axiomatic that a fixed idea and constant tendency impel to action.

False Ideal or Evil Passion
A false ideal, too, will constantly influence your will, hence its great strength. But it is the desire of an evil which is, by supposition, presented as a good (that is, disordered sexual passion, passion for gambling, intoxication, undue ambition). It does have some good as its object (pleasure, the momentary physical good of some tendency or of one of the senses). And this fixed idea is associated with remembered feelings of pleasure already experienced. It fills the field of consciousness and leaves no room for reflection upon the fact that this momentary partial good of merely one part of

your being sometimes leads to sickness, to a lasting general damage of the body. Or the pleasure is forbidden because such a false ideal involves moral evil, disease of the soul, sin. It may eventually bring on the physical, final, total evil of both soul and body in an eternity of shame.

Evil passion disunites, unbalances you by making you seek a partial good which is incapable of satisfying your instinctive tendency toward your whole good. Hence it will cause you an intimate sense of sorrow, feelings of sadness, restlessness, lack of mental control. Your personality will not be secure, but will find itself wandering astray from the path.

True Ideals
Effects of a True Ideal

A noble ideal gives unity, harmony, vigor, and fullness to life and increases the physical and mental perfection of your acts. Unity of thought and desire does away with parasite ideas, makes concentration easy, brings pleasure and maximum return to work and study.

A Latin student used to hate this subject and failed it three times. But the ideal of literature and oratory still shone brightly in his mind. So it was easy to make him understand how useful and necessary Latin is to this end. At last the hated subject was overlaid with joyful colors and in his next examination he received a very high rating.

Singleness of thought, as we said in Part 1, is not fatiguing. And because it is pleasant, it is conducive to rest. And so the ideal which makes you think steadily of what you most desire is a source of rest and joy. This is the reason, in cases of "overwork," for the effort to discover the patient's interests or ideals in order to help him to rest.

Many energies for your education and perfection are released by the ideal. The ideal of patriotism has made heroes of many timid souls. That of scholarship or research has fostered much constancy and pleasure in overcoming difficulties. The ideal of sanctity, or the priesthood, or the Christian family has preserved countless youths unspotted among the sloughs of sensuality.

The ideal of consoling Jesus Christ in His weak or sickly members has aroused and sustained holocausts of self-sacrifice and charity in asylums and hospitals. And the ideal of winning new cities and nations to Him has appealed to adventurous souls ever since the first Pentecost. Saul of Tarsus and Francis Xavier are each a colossus of heroism and superhuman grandeur, the fruits of this ideal. And they lead along behind them thousands of self-sacrificing and valiant missionaries. One aspirant to the apostolate among pagans used to say, "The ideal of my whole life is to sacrifice everything, furrow the seas, suffer everything, save one soul, then die."

As the ideal issues in a permanently vitalizing tendency, it attracts other unopposed inclinations to itself. The contrary ones it annihilates or weakens by leaving no room in the mind for the type of thought or feeling they feed upon. Your happiness increases because of this unity and exuberance of your intellectual and emotional life. You experience the natural joy of perfect acts and the profound satisfaction which follows upon merit and moral goodness.

Ignatius of Loyola fell wounded in the battle of Pamplona. His human, knightly ideal was turned into a divine ideal on contact with the *Lives of the Saints* and the *Life of Christ*. His ideal became "The greater glory of the great King." And his life was transformed into one of marvelous efficiency, unshakable peace, and superhuman heroism.

How to Choose Your Ideal

1. Choose an ideal which will not be in conflict with your total good (that is, with your final goal in life), but which will further it and make it easier to attain. Your main purpose in this life is to prepare for the next.

Caesar, Alexander the Great, and Napoleon each had an ideal of conquest which gave unity and efficiency to their lives. But the good they sought was a partial one and did not satisfy the whole soul. Moreover, it brought evil upon many peoples and nations, and was barren of happiness. All three have left us their admissions of disillusionment.

Cicero and Demosthenes had the ideal of rising in eloquence to direct their country and correct abuses. This good was ever before their eyes, ever the object of their desire. It made them overcome difficulties, attain great success, and enjoy profound satisfaction. But lower objectives filtered into their ideal, and so it did not fulfill the aspirations of their whole being.

2. Choose an ideal in agreement with your aptitudes and personality.

The Spanish historian Menéndez Pelayo considered the black legend spread throughout historical writing about Spanish Catholicism in its "Golden Age." He conceived the ideal of defending his country and religion from such great calumnies. So he studied and surpassed his colleagues in learning and elegance of style. His books astonished the world and he lived an intensely happy life while writing his marvelous

Historia de los Heterodoxos Españoles. He lived a full life and had a happy death.

3. Let your ideal be found outside of and superior to yourself. Otherwise, you could say with a famous novelist, "Charlie is a little state bounded on the north, east, south and west by Charlie." If your ideal is your body, its boundaries are limited indeed. Corruption and death come after but a few years.

The ideal of life is the development of the whole being for the profit of others and the service of God. It is the transfiguration of our instincts into a higher spiritual love. It is living in oneself and not, as it were, apart from oneself; among others and not apart from them; in God and not apart from Him (José Serre).

4. Let your ideal be practical and bring you to act at the present moment on the good thought or noble purpose you have. Do not forget that, as Lemoine puts it, "the most beautiful moment in life, the richest and most significant for the future is the present moment; at the present moment you can amend the past and construct the future." And in the present minute you can glorify the Infinite Being and by saving souls set new jewels in the divine crown of His external glory. You may say that an ideal is not perfect which cannot be realized at every instant. "If I cannot now realize my ideal," says Adela Kann, "at least I want to idealize my reality."

The greatest ideal of life is to realize at every instant the ideal of God, His most holy will. Or put it this way: to feel yourself in all things in harmony with the thought of your Creator. "The ideal of life is to live it fully and with delight," we may say with Jeglot. The ideal is to have a healthful care of one's physical life, an unlimping moral life (duty, justice, truth), a serious and orderly intellectual life, a life of the heart with a twofold movement (giving oneself and guarding oneself). The ideal is, above all, an intense spiritual life which is at the present moment clear, deep, and primarily interior. Then it will later be an apostolic one. And the ideal life should also be joyful, for service, prayer, and even suffering should enter into the great joy which is God.

5. Your ideal should be concrete and summed up in a few words to be frequently repeated.

John Berchmans understood the heroism of duty perfectly done even in the smallest affairs. "*Maximus in minimis*," he would say to himself. "I shall be outstanding in the smallest things." And he reached sanctity at the age of twenty-two. Stanislaus Kostka, hero and saint at eighteen years, made it concrete for himself thus: "I was not born for present things but for the future, for higher things (*ad altiora natus sum*)."

The Ideal of Ideals

If the infinitely perfect God were to become incarnate, this God-Man would then be the ideal of humanity.

Now it is a fact that the supreme Grandeur, unlimited Goodness, eternal Truth, infinite Beauty, God, was not only made man, our equal, companion, and model, but also willed to be the price of our ransom on the Cross, the food of our souls in the Eucharist, and our reward in Heaven.

This God-Man, with all the rights of Creator and Redeemer, of excellence, wisdom, and goodness, who wishes to reign over men and who alone offers them their greatest good in time and eternity, is not only not loved and obeyed by them all, but very many are ignorant of Him, forget and insult Him. And not a few of those who say they are His offend Him or give Him only fragments of their heart, the scraps of their love.

Yet instead of hurling sentences of condemnation He opens His breast, shows you His wounded Heart. With cries of love He says to you, "You, at least, love and console Me, make Me reign." He offers you the consoling pact He made with St. Margaret Mary: "Take care of Me and My affairs, and I shall care for you and yours." He will provide for your temporal and eternal good, your health, life, family, business, your soul, its virtues and eternal salvation. He will do this in the measure in which you give Him pleasure and glory. When you ratify this pact, all worries, scruples and phobias disappear. Your supreme good is to be taken care of by Another who understands it better than you do yourself. He wills it Himself and can procure it for you.

Elements of This Ideal

1. Surrender the past to His mercy and the future to His providence in order to live a happy life in the present. Surrender body and soul and everything to Him, for Him to care and provide for according to His will.

2. Take as your one and only ideal for every instant the giving to Him of the greatest possible pleasure by duty done, charity for your neighbor, the apostolate of souls, and fervent prayer. Summarize it thus: "Most loving King, loved and insulted, I wish always to do everything the better to love, console, and glorify You."

3. When your heart is freed from other affections, worries, and desires, give entire possession of it to "the Heart which

loves and is not loved." Enthrone Him in your heart. Make Him absolute and sovereign King of it to console Him for the sharp wound caused by chosen souls who do not receive Him or give Him only a corner of their hearts.

4. Feel His loving Presence in you by sanctifying grace, adore Him, give Him company in this living temple. Above all, consult His desires and ask His orders. Let Him reign in your senses, faculties, feelings, and works.

Effects of This Ideal

There are wonderful promises made to those truly devoted to His Heart. They will have blessings on all their undertakings, peace, fervor, sanctity, eternal salvation, an effective apostolate.

1. Mentally you will obtain the change of sorrow into joy. You will see suffering as very attractive since the King, Infinite Wisdom, chose suffering for Himself. Crowned with thorns, He Himself asks for victims to help Him by voluntary suffering to placate the justice of God and save souls.

2. You will obtain the unification of your life through this sublime ideal. It is an ideal which is realizable at each and every moment. You will overcome that bothersome duality of mental life, phobias, worries, and subjective sorrow.

3. You will obtain a consoling fullness of your intellectual and emotional life by knowing, loving, and possessing Infinite Truth and Goodness. This will happen in a most attractive and intimate manner, that is, by the God-Man dwelling within you, opening His breast to show you His Heart, impatient with love for you and struck by sorrow when you do not permit Him to give you even greater gifts.

Such a happy person as this, dominated by the interests and person of Him who takes possession of it and reigns completely in its depths, who communicates to it His own peace, happiness, and life, is like the clear, crystal water of a quiet lake. Human events will, like gentle breezes, scarcely trouble the surface of the water and will not disturb the clear image of blue sky, symbol of divine peace and happiness, which are common to both hearts, the throne-heart and the Heart Enthroned.

Choice of an Ideal Vision for One's Life

False ideal
- Idea, tendency and will fixed upon evil
- This causes turbulence and disunion

True Ideal

Effects
- Unifies and harmonizes life
- Gives concentration and efficiency
- Helps rest and enjoyment
- Perfects and dignifies

Choice of an ideal
- In harmony with your ultimate end
- Conformed to your aptitudes
- Outside of and superior to yourself
- Practicable, realizable at every instant
- Make it concrete in a few words

Ideal of ideals, Christ the King

Object
- Most noble: the ideal Man
- Most lovable: Love that is not loved
- Most useful: that He might reign in all men

Concrete
- Contract, unconditional surrender
- He will take care of you
- "Whatever pleases Him more"
- Motive: to love and console Him
- Method: make Him King of your heart and accompany Him, obey Him, identify yourself with Him and His interests

Effects

Spiritual — His promises
- Peace, fervor
- blessing, salvation
- Effective apostolate

Mental
- Unification of life
- Change of sorrow into joy
- Killing of phobias
- Consoling fullness of life of — Intellect / Feelings

16

Résumé
Directives for Health and Efficiency

1. Be conscious of your mental and bodily capital. Recognize the limitations of your strength. If this has been depleted by an extraordinary or prolonged effort, know how to replenish it in time by proportionate rest. Do not prolong concentration of attention for more than two hours without a few minutes of conscious sensations and muscular relaxation. The sick, weak, and convalescent should abbreviate their effort all the more.

2. Do your job or everyday duty with the greatest possible perfection, that is, with concentration, naturalness, and pleasure. Avoid all tension, haste, and disgust. Find in your work the strength and joy of an ideal. *"Age quod agis,"* "Do what you're doing."

3. Do not try to realize at the instant *all* the good and greatness to which your impulses urge you, but only what is possible *at the time* and which a tranquil judgment shows you is proportioned to your abilities.

4. In time of relaxation avoid exaggerated competition. Recognize and accept the physical, intellectual, and moral superiority

of others. If you must be pre-eminent in something, let it be in goodness, understanding, and patience.

5. In time of failure or adversity, know how to find and how to reflect on the goodness or usefulness this offers for yourself or others, for time or for eternity. Set this counterweight against excessive sadness and discouragement. Accept the inevitable and base your ideal upon it. This will be the secret of your efficiency and happiness.

6. Avoid the tension which comes from doubt and insecurity about your health, skill, and temporal or eternal success. Trust in your strength and divine aid. Let religious faith and tranquillity of conscience be your guarantee.

7. Make use of the greatest of your faculties by means of deliberate, concrete, and motivated decisions. Then put them into execution without fatigue or further discussion. This will give you a strong and healthy personality.

8. Recognize the double tendency in you: the angel and the beast. Make the higher level of life control and rule the lower levels. Make the good of your whole being keep its supremacy over sense pleasure, caprice, or the good of a single part.

Sophia Institute

Sophia Institute is a nonprofit institution that seeks to nurture the spiritual, moral, and cultural life of souls and to spread the gospel of Christ in conformity with the authentic teachings of the Roman Catholic Church.

Sophia Institute Press fulfills this mission by offering translations, reprints, and new publications that afford readers a rich source of the enduring wisdom of mankind.

Sophia Institute also operates the popular online resource CatholicExchange.com. *Catholic Exchange* provides world news from a Catholic perspective as well as daily devotionals and articles that will help readers to grow in holiness and live a life consistent with the teachings of the Church.

In 2013, Sophia Institute launched Sophia Institute for Teachers to renew and rebuild Catholic culture through service to Catholic education. With the goal of nurturing the spiritual, moral, and cultural life of souls, and an abiding respect for the role and work of teachers, we strive to provide materials and programs that are at once enlightening to the mind and ennobling to the heart; faithful and complete, as well as useful and practical.

Sophia Institute gratefully recognizes the Solidarity Association for preserving and encouraging the growth of our apostolate over the course of many years. Without their generous and timely support, this book would not be in your hands.

www.SophiaInstitute.com
www.CatholicExchange.com
www.SophiaInstituteforTeachers.org

Sophia Institute Press® is a registered trademark of Sophia Institute. Sophia Institute is a tax-exempt institution as defined by the Internal Revenue Code, Section 501(c)(3). Tax ID 22-2548708.